THE CHRISTIAN'S WALK

A Practical Study for the Christian's Lifestyle

Study Guide
Teacher's Edition

Jeremy Markle

WALKING IN THE WORD MINISTRIES

Jeremy Markle
www.walkinginthewordministries.net

THE CHRISTIAN'S WALK

A Practical Study for the Christian's Lifestyle

Study Guide
Teacher's Edition

All rights reserved solely by the author.
No part of this book may be reproduced, stored in a retrieval system,
or transmitted in any form or by any means –
electronic, mechanical, photocopy, recording, or otherwise –
without written permission of the author.

Unless otherwise noted, all Scripture quotations are from the King James Version.

Copyright © 2023 by Jeremy Markle

Published by Walking in the WORD Ministries
www.walkinginthewordministries.net

Printed in the United States of America

ISBN: 978-1-947430-41-9

Content

Walking in Jesus Christ
      Walking by Faith .... Study Guide - Page 1

Walking Worthy
    Walking Worthy of God
    Walking Worthy of the Lord
    Walking Worthy of the Vocation................. Study Guide - Page 23

Walking in Newness of Life
      Walking as a New Creature..................... Study Guide - Page 43

Walking in Good Works .... Study Guide - Page 61

Walking in the Light
    Walking in Love
    Walking in Truth
    Walking Circumspectly
    Walking after Commandments .... Study Guide - Page 81

Walking in the Spirit .... Study Guide - Page 105

Walking Where You Are Called
    Walking in the Fear of the Lord
    Walking According to the Gospel .... Study Guide - Page 127

Walking with Them That Are Without................. Study Guide - Page 147

Walking after an Example
    Walking by the Same Rule
    Walking with the Same Mind
    Walking in the Same Spirit .... Study Guide - Page 167

Walking in Abundance .... Study Guide - Page 183

I John 2:6

He that saith he abideth in him ought himself also so to walk, even as he walked.

An Introduction to the Christian's Walk

At the end of His earthly ministry, Jesus called his disciples together and gave them His final command for their lives and ministries. Matthew 28:18-20 records Jesus saying, "***All power is given unto me in heaven and in earth. Go ye therefore, and teach all nations, baptizing them in the name of the Father, and of the Son, and of the Holy Ghost: Teaching them to observe all things whatsoever I have commanded you: and, lo, I am with you alway, even unto the end of the world. Amen.***" Jesus had a specific purpose and plan for His disciples in His absence. They were to represent Him to the world around them by teaching the nations of His Gospel of salvation, baptizing those who believed as a public testimony of their faith and then teaching the believers to observe, or put into practice, His teachings (Mark 16:15-16).

In Bible times, the title *disciple* was given to students of a religious teacher. It was expected that such students would not simply learn the information that their teacher provided but also that they would "*observe*" or diligently apply that teaching to their daily lives so that they would begin to live like him (Matthew 28:20). That is why the apostle John recorded Jesus as saying "***to those Jews which believed on him, If ye continue in my word, then are ye my disciples indeed***" (John 8:31). He later added, "***By this shall all men know that ye are my disciples, if ye have love one to another***" (John 13:35). Finally, He stated, "***Herein is my Father glorified, that ye bear much fruit; so shall ye be my disciples***" (John 15:8). Jesus expects all those who believe on Him to become His disciples by learning and living according to His Word, displaying His love, and glorifying God the Father by allowing Him to produce spiritual fruit in their lives (Luke 14:21-33).

One of the primary words used in the New Testament and within Christianity today to describe how a disciple of Jesus Christ is to "*observe*" His commandments is the word *walk*. In this context the word *walk* takes on its figurative meaning of making consistent choices, based on one's beliefs, that form a direction of life for either good or evil, resulting in a habitual lifestyle.

It is the purpose of this Bible study to address the forty-seven uses of the word *walk* in their thirty-two passages, to highlight ten specific biblical truths that should be applied to each believer's daily activities so that the believer can truly be one of Christ's disciples and represent Him to the world.

Chapter I

Walking in Jesus Christ
Walking by Faith

Colossians 2:1-12
6 As ye have therefore received Christ Jesus the Lord,
so walk ye in him:
7 Rooted and built up in him,
and stablished in the faith,
as ye have been taught,
abounding therein with thanksgiving.

Romans 4:8-25
11 ...that he might be the father of all them that
believe,
...that righteousness might be imputed unto them also:
12 ...who also walk in the steps of that faith
of our father Abraham

II Corinthians 5:7
7 (For we walk by faith, not by sight:)

I John 2:4-6
6 He that saith he abideth in him
ought himself also so to walk,
even as he walked.

Chapter 1

Walking in Jesus Christ
Walking by Faith

Colossians 2:1-12
Romans 4:8-25
II Corinthians 5:7
I John 2:4-6

Biblical Instruction about Walking in Jesus Christ

In Colossians 2:6, the apostle Paul commanded believers to walk in Christ, saying, "***As ye have therefore received Christ Jesus the Lord, so walk ye in him***." Although walking in Christ may sound difficult, it is not. Paul specifically began his command with the words, "***as ye have***," indicating that walking in Christ is a continuation of what every believer has already done to receive Him as their personal Savior. It is to "***walk by faith, not by sight***" (II Corinthians 5:7). Just as you have trusted in Christ to forgive you of your sins and to give you eternal life without having personally seen Him on the cross or risen from the tomb, so you must allow His Word to guide your daily living. For "***faith cometh by hearing, and hearing by the word of God***" (Romans 10:17). *Walking in Christ is a lifestyle that lives by faith in Him and learns from His Word.*

Walking in Jesus Christ Begins with Faith in His Salvation and Sufficiency

In Colossians 1:4, Paul testified that he had *"heard of [the believer's] faith in Christ Jesus"* for salvation. He further praised the believers in Colossians 2:5, saying, *"For though I be absent in the flesh, yet am I with you in the spirit, joying and beholding your order, and the stedfastness of your faith in Christ."* The believers in Colosse had begun their new life in Christ well by *"walk[ing] in the steps of that faith of our father Abraham,"* by receiving *"the righteousness of faith"* (Romans 4:12-13). They could say with Paul, *"Yea doubtless, and I count all things but loss for the excellency of the knowledge of Christ Jesus my Lord.... And be found in him, not having mine own righteousness, which is of the law, but that which is through the faith of Christ, the righteousness which is of God by faith: That I may know him..."* (Philippians 3:8-10).

Although Paul knew of the believers' faith in Christ for salvation, he was very concerned that false teachers and worldly men would *"beguile [them] with enticing words"* and discourage or distract them from their faith in Christ in other areas of their life (Colossians 2:4). He then warned them by saying, *"Beware lest any man spoil you through philosophy and vain deceit, after the tradition of men, after the rudiments of the world, and not after Christ"* (Colossians 2:8). He also said, *"Let no man beguile you of your reward in a voluntary humility and worshipping of angels, intruding into those things which he hath not seen, vainly puffed up by his fleshly mind"* (Colossians 2:18). Paul knew that worldly temptations and man-made religious activities could be appealing. He also knew that they rob believers of the true satisfaction that is only found in Christ. Therefore, he reassured them by saying, while speaking of God the Father and Christ, *"In whom are hid all the treasures of wisdom and knowledge"* (Colossians 2:3). He added, while speaking specifically of Christ, *"For in him dwelleth all the fulness of the Godhead bodily. And ye are complete in him, which is the head of all principality and power"* (Colossians 2:9-10). As you, like the believers in Paul's day, walk in Christ by "***Looking unto Jesus the author and finisher of our faith,***" you are guaranteed all the wisdom and knowledge needed for each day of your life as He completes you (Hebrews 12:1-3; see also II Peter 1:2-4, James 1:5-8). Christ *was* sufficient to save you from your sins and *is* sufficient to lead you in every other area of your daily life.

Walking in Jesus Christ Is a Continual Process

Following Paul's warning and instruction, he provided four spiritual requirements that each believer must continually fulfill to walk in Christ by faith. He said in Colossians 2:6-7, "***As ye have therefore received Christ Jesus the Lord, so walk ye in him: Rooted and built up in him, and stablished in the faith, as ye have been taught, abounding therein with thanksgiving.***"

First, you must be firmly "***rooted…in him,***" or secure in your relationship with Christ as your personal Savior. It is for this reason that Paul said to the believers in Colosse, "***And you, that were sometime alienated and enemies in your mind by wicked works, yet now hath he reconciled in the body of his flesh through death, to present you holy and unblameable and unreproveable in his sight: If ye continue in the faith grounded and settled, and be not moved away from the hope of the gospel, which ye have heard…***" (Colossians 1:21-23). Satan knows that if he can lead you to doubt your salvation from your sin, you will be hindered in your daily walk with Christ. However, God does not want you to go through life with doubts about your salvation or about His love. Paul is reminding you that before you trusted Christ as your Savior you committed "***wicked works,***" but now that Christ has paid for your sins through His death, you can live "***holy and unblameable and unreproveable in his sight***" as you focus on the change He has made in your life through the "***the hope of the Gospel***" (Colossians 1:21-23; see also I Corinthians 15:1-4). Just as a new plant must push its roots deep into the soil to find nutrients and strength, so you must continually deepen your dependence and knowledge of Christ through His Word so that you are secure in your daily spiritual life (Psalms 1:1-6). Jesus said, "*Therefore whosoever heareth these sayings of mine, and doeth them, I will liken him unto a wise man, which built his house upon a rock: And the rain descended, and the floods came, and the winds blew, and beat upon that house; and it fell not: for it was founded upon a rock. And every one that heareth these sayings of mine, and doeth them not, shall be likened unto a foolish man, which built his house upon the sand: And the rain descended, and the floods came, and the winds blew, and beat upon that house; and it fell: and great was the fall of it*" (Matthew 7:24-27; see also James 1:22-25).

Second, you must be "***built up in him***," or growing in your relationship with Christ. It is natural for a plant that has deep roots to begin to grow upward as it begins to fulfill its purpose of producing good fruit. Jesus taught this truth to a multitude through a lengthy but important parable, saying, "*Hearken; Behold, there went out a sower to sow: And it came to pass, as he sowed, some fell by the way side, and the fowls of the air came and devoured it up. And some fell on stony ground, where it had not much earth; and immediately it sprang up, because it had no depth of earth: But when the sun was up, it was scorched; and because it had no root, it withered away. And some fell among thorns, and the thorns grew up, and choked it, and it yielded no fruit. And other fell on good ground, and did yield fruit that sprang up and increased; and brought forth, some thirty, and some sixty, and some an hundred.... The sower soweth the word. And these are they by the way side, where the word is sown; but when they have heard, Satan cometh immediately, and taketh away the word that was sown in their hearts. And these are they likewise which are sown on stony ground; who, when they have heard the word, immediately receive it with gladness; And have no root in themselves, and so endure but for a time: afterward, when affliction or persecution ariseth for the word's sake, immediately they are offended. And these are they which are sown among thorns; such as hear the word, and the cares of this world, and the deceitfulness of riches, and the lusts of other things entering in, choke the word, and it becometh unfruitful. And these are*

The Christian's Walk

they which are sown on good ground; such as hear the word, and receive it, and bring forth fruit, some thirtyfold, some sixty, and some an hundred" (Mark 4:3-20).

In this parable, Jesus revealed that although all four types of people heard the Word of God, only one produced a bountiful harvest. One group heard God's Word with their ears but rejected it in their heart. Two groups heard God's Word and initially received it, but later allowed circumstances to distract or discourage them from faithfully applying it. Only the group that heard God's Word and applied its teaching to their lives brought forth the fruit that God desired to produce in them.

Third, you must be "*stablished in the faith, as ye have been taught,*" or steadfast in the Scriptural instruction that you have received from other believers and the local church. God, in His perfect wisdom and love, has not left you all alone to figure out your Christian life. He has created the local church, where believers can gather together to hear God's Word be taught and encourage each other in their life of faith. Paul explained that the spiritual leadership in the local church was specifically given "*for the perfecting [or maturing] of the saints, for the work of the ministry, for the edifying of the body of Christ: Till we all come in the unity of the faith, and of the knowledge of the Son of God, unto a perfect man, unto the measure of the stature of the fulness of Christ: That we henceforth be no more children, tossed to and fro, and carried about with every wind of doctrine, by the sleight of men, and cunning craftiness, whereby they lie in wait to deceive; but speaking the truth in love, may grow up into him in all things, which is the head, even Christ: From whom the whole body fitly joined together and compacted by that which every joint supplieth, according to the effectual working in the measure of every part, maketh increase of the body unto the edifying of itself in love*" (Ephesians 4:12-16). The local church is a place of refuge from the world, where sinners, saved by Christ, can work together to know Him better and protect each other from sin's influences. It is for this reason that Hebrews 10:23-25 says, "*Let us hold fast the profession of our faith without wavering; (for he is faithful that promised;) And let us consider one another to provoke unto love and to good works: Not forsaking the assembling of ourselves together, as the manner of some is; but exhorting one another: and so much the more, as ye see the day approaching."*

However, it is important for you to understand that Paul did not say you must simply hear the teaching of God's Word, but rather that you must be steadfast in your faith based on the truths that are taught. The Bible addresses every topic necessary for the Christian's life. Those topics are called the doctrines, or teachings, of the faith. They do not replace your faith in Christ but rather are the truths that He wants you to learn and apply to your life after you are saved so that you can live like Him. I John 2:6 says, "***He that saith he abideth in him ought himself also so to walk, even as he walked.***" The purpose of the local church and other faithful believers in your life is to help you learn and then live what God has revealed in His Word so that you might "***put ye on the Lord Jesus Christ, and make not provision for the flesh, to fulfil the lusts thereof***" (Romans 13:14).

Fourth, you must be "***abounding therein with thanksgiving,***" or consistently increasing in your gratitude for your salvation and God's instruction for your new walk in Christ. As a believer in Jesus, there is much for which to be thankful. Paul reminded the believers at Colosse of just a few, saying "***Giving thanks unto the Father, which hath made us meet to be partakers of the inheritance of the saints in light: who hath delivered us from the power of darkness, and hath translated us into the kingdom of his dear Son: in whom we have redemption through his blood, even the forgiveness of sins***" (Colossians 1:12-14). Later he wrote to them, saying, "***And let the peace of God rule in your hearts, to the which also ye are called in one body; and be ye thankful. Let the word of Christ dwell in you richly in all wisdom; teaching and admonishing one another in psalms and hymns and spiritual songs, singing with grace in your hearts to the Lord. And whatsoever ye do in word or deed, do all in the name of the Lord Jesus, giving thanks to God and*** *the Father by him.*" (Colossians 3:15-17) Godly gratitude will protect you from discouragements and distractions presented to you by life's circumstances and the world's temptations. You must remember the goodness of God in the past and His precious promises for the future so that you can trust Him in the present. For you are to "*in every thing give thanks: for this is the will of God in Christ Jesus concerning you*" (I Thessalonians 5:18).

Walking in Jesus Christ Is a Personal Choice
    Are you walking in Christ? Have you placed your faith in Him for the forgiveness of your sins and received His eternal salvation? Are you trusting Jesus, not only for your salvation, but also to be sufficient to guide you through every other area of your Christian life? Are you frequently remembering the significance of the Gospel and changes it brought to your life? Are you growing in your relationship with Christ? Are you learning and living Scriptural truths that are making you steadfast in your faith and Christ-like in your living? If you are struggling in any of the above areas, why not share your need with God in prayer right now and ask Him to forgive you of any sin, to guide you by His Word, and to encourage you through fellow Christians so that you can live like Christ and be protected from the discouragements and distractions that regularly confront you.

The Christian's Walk

Biblical Principles about Walking in Jesus Christ

- ✓ **Ephesians 2:8-9** - Salvation is by faith alone–not works.

- ✓ **Hebrews 10:36** - The just live by faith, and God has no pleasure in those without faith.

- ✓ **Hebrews 11:1-40** - Many have lived by faith and have been rewarded by God.

- ✓ **Romans 16:17-18** - Wrong doctrine and those that teach it must be avoided.

- ✓ **I Corinthians 1:29-31** - Jesus Christ is sufficient to be each Christian's wisdom, righteousness, sanctification, and redemption.

- ✓ **II Peter 3:18** - Christians are to grow in their knowledge of Jesus Christ.

- ✓ **I Corinthians 3:9-15** - Christians build their lives on the foundation of Jesus Christ, and what they build will be tested by fire in heaven.

- ✓ **II Timothy 3:14-17** - The Bible was given by God for the purpose of teaching Christians how to live a mature life full of good works.

- ✓ **Matthew 16:18-19** - Jesus Christ is the founder of the church.

Walking in Jesus Christ

- ✓ **I Corinthians 12:12-27** - God has made the local church to work like a body; each member is needed and is to care for the other.

- ✓ **Romans 8:29** - God is working to conform each Christian to the image of Jesus Christ.

- ✓ **Ephesians 4:20-24** - Learning from Jesus Christ will teach each Christian to put off his old man and put on his new man in holiness.

- ✓ **Colossians 3:17** - Everything that a Christian does should be done with thanksgiving.

- ✓ **Hebrews 13:15** - Christians should be continually giving thanks to God.

- ✓ _____ - _____
- ✓ _____ - _____
- ✓ _____ - _____
- ✓ _____ - _____
- ✓ _____ - _____
- ✓ _____ - _____

Biblical Investigation about Walking in Jesus Christ

✎ Bible Reading: Colossians 2:1-12, Romans 4:8-12, II Corinthians 5:7, I John 2:4-6

✎ Bible Memory Verses: Colossians 2:6-7

6 As ye have therefore received Christ Jesus the Lord, so walk ye in him:
7 Rooted and built up in him, and stablished in the faith, as ye have been taught, abounding therein with thanksgiving.

1. Walking in Jesus Christ is a lifestyle that <u>lives</u> by <u>faith</u> in Him and <u>learns</u> from His <u>Word</u>.

2. How must you walk if you are going to walk in Jesus Christ? (Colossians 2:6)
   <u>By Faith</u>

3. Is faith believing what you see, or trusting in what you cannot see? (II Corinthians 5:7, Hebrews 11:1)
   <u>Trusting what I cannot see</u>

4. On what must your faith be based? (Romans 10:17)
   <u>The Word of God</u>
   ☞ Are you regularly hearing and reading the Word of God so that your faith can increase?

   How can you improve your Bible reading?

Walking in Jesus Christ
Begins with Faith in His Salvation and Sufficiency

5. When did you accept Jesus Christ as your personal Savior by faith? (Colossians 1:4, 2:5)
   _____
   _____

   ☞ If you have not yet accepted Jesus Christ as your personal Savior, would you like to do so now? You can express your faith in Christ in a short prayer admitting that you are a sinner and asking God to forgive you based on your faith in Jesus Christ, and He will do so freely. Then share your decision with your pastor or the Christian who has shared this Bible study with you.

6. Whose example did you follow when you placed your faith in Jesus Christ as your Savior? (Romans 4:12-13)
   Abraham's

7. What was Paul willing to sacrifice in order to know Jesus Christ? (Philippians 3:7-10)
   Everything
   ☞ Are you willing to make the same sacrifice so that you can know Jesus Christ?

   What did God give you when you placed your faith in Jesus Christ as your personal Savior?
   Righteousness

8. Why was Paul concerned for the believers in Colosse (Colossians 2:4, 8, 18)

4 And this I say, lest any man should <u>beguile</u> you with <u>enticing words</u>.
8 Beware lest any man <u>spoil</u> you through <u>philosophy</u> and <u>vain deceit</u>, after the tradition of <u>men</u>, after the rudiments of the <u>world</u>, and not after Christ.
18 Let no man <u>beguile</u> you of your reward in a voluntary humility and worshipping of angels, intruding into those things which he hath not seen, vainly puffed up by his fleshly mind,

☞ How might you be influenced by man's philosophies rather than by Jesus Christ's truths?

9. In Whom can you find true wisdom and knowledge? (Colossians 2:1-3)
God the Father and Jesus Christ

10. Who makes you truly complete? (Colossians 2:9-10, John 10:10)
Jesus Christ
☞ What are some ways the world might offer you false completion?

11. Who is the author and finisher of your faith? (Hebrews 12:1-3; see also II Peter 1:2-4, James 1:5-8)
Jesus Christ
☞ What are some ways that you can keep your eyes on Jesus Christ?

What will happen if you do not keep your eyes on Jesus Christ?
I will become weary and faint in my mind.

Walking in Jesus Christ
Is a Continual Process

12. What are the four spiritual conditions that you must fulfill in order to keep yourself walking in Jesus Christ by faith? (Colossians 2:6-7)
    a   _Be rooted in Jesus Christ_
    b   _Be built up in Jesus Christ_
    c   _Be established in faith through teaching_
    d   _Be thankful_

13. What types of works did you do before you were reconciled by Jesus Christ's death? (Colossians 1:21-23)
    Wicked works
    How does God see you after you have accepted Christ's payment for your sins?
    Holy, unblameable, and unreproveable
    Where must your hope/faith be grounded if you are going to be established in Jesus Christ?
    In the Gospel

14. What is the Gospel? (I Corinthians 15:1-4)
1 Moreover, brethren, I declare unto you the gospel which I preached unto you, which also you have received, and wherein ye stand;
2 by which also ye are <u>saved</u>, if ye keep in memory what I preached unto you, unless ye have believed in vain.
3 For I delivered unto you first of all that which I also received, how that Christ <u>died</u> for our sins according to the scriptures;
4 and that he was <u>buried</u>, and that he <u>rose again</u> the third day according to the scriptures:

15. What two things must you do with God's Word if you are going to have true security throughout your life? (Matthew 7:24-27, Psalms 1:1-6, James 1:22-25)
    a   <u>Hear it</u>
    b   <u>Do it</u>

16. In Jesus Christ's parable about the four souls/hearts, what does the seed represent? (Mark 4:3-20)
    <u>The Word of God</u>
    Why did the first soil/heart not receive the seed that was sown?
    <u>Its soil/heart was hard, and Satan took the seed away.</u>

    Why did the second soil/heart not produce fruit?
    <u>It had no roots and was offended due to the afflictions and persecution brought about by the Word.</u>
    Why did the third soil/heart not produce fruit?
    <u>It allowed the cares of this world, the deceitfulness of riches, and the lusts of other things to choke out the Word.</u>
    Why did the fourth soil/heart produce an abundance of fruit?
    <u>It heard the Word and received the Word.</u>

☞ How have you been responding to the Word of God, and must you make any changes so that you can produce spiritual fruit?

17. What are some of the reasons that God has given you a local church and its spiritual leadership? (Ephesians 4:12-16)
    a   To prepare me for ministry

    b   To help me edify the body of Jesus Christ (other believers)

    c   To help me be united with other believers in the faith and the knowledge of Jesus Christ
    d   To protect me from false doctrines and teachings of men

    e   To help me by speaking the truth in love

18. What will regularly attending and participating in your local church help you to do with your faith? (Hebrews 10:23-25)
    Hold fast to my profession of faith
    What will regularly attending and participating in your local church help you to accomplish?
    Good works
    What should you do to other Christians while attending your local church?
    Exhort them
    ☞ Are you willing to commit to attending your local church for each of its weekly services so that you can fulfill the above goals? If not, why not?

19. If you say that you are abiding in Jesus Christ by faith, how should you be walking/living? (I John 2:6)
    <u>Like Him</u>

20. Why should you be abounding with thanksgiving toward God? (Colossians 1:12-14; see also Colossians 3:15-17)
    12 giving thanks unto the Father, which hath made us meet to be <u>partakers</u> of the <u>inheritance</u> of the saints in light:
    13 who hath <u>delivered</u> us from the power of <u>darkness</u>, and hath <u>translated</u> us into the kingdom of his dear <u>Son</u>:
    14 in whom we have <u>redemption</u> through his blood, even the <u>forgiveness</u> of sins:

21. In how many of life's circumstances should you be thankful? (I Thessalonians 5:18)
    <u>In everything</u>
    List a few things for which you are thankful.
    _____
    _____
    _____
    _____

Walking in Jesus Christ
Is a Personal Choice

22. Are there areas of your life that you should change so you can be walking in Jesus Christ? What are those areas, and what changes should you make? Will you ask God for His help to make these changes?

Personal Notes about Walking in Jesus Christ

Chapter 2

Walking Worthy
Walking Worthy of God
Walking Worthy of the Lord
Walking Worthy of the Vocation

I Thessalonians 2:10-12
11 As you know how we exhorted and comforted and
charged every one of you, as a father doth his children,
12 That ye would walk worthy of God, who hath called
you unto his kingdom and glory.

Colossians 1:9-14
9 For this cause we also, since the day we heard it,
do not cease to pray for you, and to desire...
10 That ye might walk worthy of the Lord
unto all pleasing,
being fruitful in every good work,
and increasing in the knowledge of God;

Ephesians 4:1-3
1 I therefore, the prisoner of the Lord,
beseech you that ye walk worthy of the vocation
wherewith ye are called,
2 With all lowliness and meekness, with longsuffering,
forbearing one another in love;
3 Endeavouring to keep the unity of the Spirit
in the bond of peace.

Chapter 2

Walking Worthy
Walking Worthy of God
Walking Worthy of the Lord
Walking Worthy of Your Spiritual Vocation

I Thessalonians 2:10-12
Colossians 1:9-14
Ephesians 4:1-4

Biblical Instruction about Walking Worthy

On three occasions in the New Testament, believers are instructed to *"walk worthy,"* or to live a life that realistically reflects the value of someone or something (I Thessalonians 2:10-12, Colossians 1:9-14, Ephesians 4:1-4). For you to fulfill such instruction, you must first recognize the value of the object you are to reflect and then determine to live in such a way that the person or object's value is not diminished. *Walking worthy is a lifestyle that recognizes and then reflects another person's or object's value.* As a Christian, you must recognize and reflect the value of God, the Lord Jesus Christ, and your spiritual vocation.

Walking Worthy of God the Father

In I Thessalonians 2:10-12, the apostle Paul lovingly instructed the believers in Thessalonica to *"walk worthy of God."* Paul could only spend a few weeks with the Thessalonian believers before he was forced to leave due to persecution. For this reason, he was not correcting them, but *"as a father doth his*

Walking Worthy

children," he *"exhorted and comforted"* them (I Thessalonians 2:11). Then he *"charged,"* or taught, them how to begin living out their new relationship with God, their heavenly Father, through their faith in Christ as their personal Savior (I Thessalonians 2:11).

God the Father's attributes, character, strength, and glory have value beyond human comprehension. In Job 9:10, Job testified that God *"doeth great things past finding out; yea, and wonders without number."* In Psalm 29:1-2, King David praised God by saying, *"Give unto the LORD, O ye mighty, Give unto the LORD glory and strength. Give unto the LORD the glory due unto his name; Worship the LORD in the beauty of holiness."* In Revelation 4:8-11, the apostle John recorded that the heavenly beings praise God as they *"rest not day and night, saying, Holy, holy, holy, Lord God Almighty, which was, and is, and is to come. And when those beasts give glory and honour and thanks to him that sat on the throne, who liveth for ever and ever, the four and twenty elders fall down before him that sat on the throne, and worship him that liveth for ever and ever, and cast their crowns before the throne, saying, Thou art worthy, O Lord, to receive glory and honour and power: for thou hast created all things, and for thy pleasure they are and were created."* God's value is without human calculation, yet Christians are to walk worthy of His value by reflecting Him in their day-to-day living.

Although the task of walking worthy of God may seem impossible, it is no more impossible than a little boy trying to grow up to be like his daddy by copying his example. Paul encouraged the believers in Thessalonica to remember his example of godly living by saying, *"Ye are witnesses, and God also, how holily and justly and unblameably we behaved ourselves among you that believe"* (I Thessalonians 2:10). Paul was a sinner saved by God's grace just as you are. Yet, because he valued God as his heavenly Father, he *"behaved"* himself in such a way that God's holiness, justice, and blamelessness were reflected in his daily activities. The apostle Peter said it this way: *"As obedient children, not fashioning yourselves according to the former lusts in your ignorance: But as he which hath called you is holy, so be ye holy in all manner of conversation; Because it is written, Be ye holy; for I am holy*" (I Peter 1:14-16). Therefore, if you, like the believers in Thessalonica, are going to walk worthy of God, you must purposefully separate yourself from sinful attitudes and actions that you know go against your heavenly Father's likeness.

Paul followed up his instruction to the Thessalonian believers by motivating them—and you— to walk worthy of God because He "*hath called you unto his kingdom and glory*" (I Thessalonians 2:12). God, in His divine love, chose to allow you to be part of His eternal kingdom and to enjoy His glory through the Gospel of Jesus Christ (Colossians 1:13). For this reason, you should naturally value Him and desire to reflect His value in your style of living. Peter wrote, "*But ye are a chosen generation, a royal priesthood, an holy nation, a peculiar people; that ye should shew forth the praises of him who hath called you out of darkness into his marvellous light: Which in time past were not a people, but are now the people of God: which had not obtained mercy, but now have obtained mercy*" (I Peter 2:9-10).

Walking Worthy of the Lord Jesus Christ

In Colossians 1:9-14, Paul shared his prayer for the believers in Colosse. In verse nine, he prayed that they would "*be filled with the knowledge of [Jesus Christ's] will*" for their lives. Then, in verse ten, he prayed that they would practically apply that knowledge, saying, "*That ye might walk worthy of the Lord unto all pleasing*" (Colossians 1:10). The Colossian believers had expressed their faith in Christ as their personal Savior. Yet, they still needed to commit themselves to reflect Him in their day-to-day activities so that He might be pleased with the results. You need to make the same commitment.

Paul presented four specific ways in which believers can please Christ in their daily walk. The first is by "*being fruitful in every good work*" (Colossians 1:10). Although salvation does not come by doing good works, Christ "*gave himself for us, that he might redeem us from all iniquity, and purify unto himself a peculiar people, zealous of good works*" (Titus 2:14). When you commit to doing that which you know is right according to God's Word, you are pleasing to Christ and demonstrating that you are walking in Him.

Second, you can walk worthy of and please Christ by "*increasing in the knowledge of God*" (Colossians 1:10). Jesus said, "*This is life eternal, that they might know thee the only true God, and Jesus Christ, whom thou hast sent*" (John 17:3). God desires that you begin enjoying the benefits of your eternal life while still living here on earth. In heaven, you will have everything you will ever need supplied for you by God, and the same is true here on earth. Remember that in lesson one, we discovered that Peter said, "*Grace and peace be multiplied unto you through the knowledge of God, and of Jesus our Lord, according as his divine power hath given unto us all things that pertain unto life and godliness, through the knowledge of him that hath called us to glory and virtue*" (II Peter 1:2-3). When you commit to growing in your knowledge of and relationship with God the Father, you are pleasing to Christ and demonstrating that you are walking in Him.

Third, you can walk worthy and please Christ when you are "*strengthened with all might, according to his glorious power, unto all patience and longsuffering with joyfulness*" (Colossians 1:11). Christ does not expect you to live the Christian life in your own power. Instead, He freely offers His all-sufficient power to help you with each event in your life. Paul, after facing many responsibilities and trials, testified that he was empowered by Christ, saying, "*I can do all things through Christ which strengtheneth me*" (Philippians 4:13). When you commit to depend on Christ for the strength to accomplish each day's tasks, you will find greater patience with others, longsuffering in adverse circumstances, and joyfulness in the outcome (II Corinthians 12:7-10). You will also be pleasing to Him as you continually walk in Him.

The Christian's Walk

Fourth, you can walk worthy and please Christ when you are *"**giving thanks unto the Father, which hath made us meet to be partakers of the inheritance of the saints in light**"* (Colossians 1:12). Life on this earth has many disappointments that can cause you to become discouraged and complain. But when you remember that your future inheritance from God, Who is your heavenly Father, is *"**incorruptible, and undefiled, and fadeth not away, reserved in heaven for you,**"* you should be filled with gratitude and say, *"**Blessed be the God and Father of our Lord Jesus Christ, which according to his abundant mercy hath begotten us again unto a lively hope**"* (I Peter 1:3-5). Such a view will not remove the disappointments of this life, but can make your hope of heaven much more wonderful and your thanksgiving to God that much more profound. As Peter said, *"**Seeing then that all these things shall be dissolved, what manner of persons ought ye to be in all holy conversation and godliness, looking for and hasting unto the coming of the day of God, wherein the heavens being on fire shall be dissolved, and the elements shall melt with fervent heat? Nevertheless we, according to his promise, look for new heavens and a new earth, wherein dwelleth righteousness**"* (II Peter 3:11-13). When you commit to giving thanks to God regularly for His blessing of eternity in heaven, you are pleasing to Christ and are demonstrating that you are walking in Him.

Walking Worthy of Your Spiritual Vocation

In Ephesians 4:1-4, Paul pleaded with the believers in Ephesus to *"**walk worthy of the vocation wherewith ye are called.**"* As with the believers in Thessalonica and Colosse, Paul was not scolding them for doing wrong in the past but instead was encouraging them to do what was right in the future. As Paul began his letter, he reminded the believers of God's great love for them, saying, *"**Blessed be the God and Father of our Lord Jesus Christ, who hath blessed us with all spiritual blessings in heavenly places in Christ: According as he hath chosen us in him before the foundation of the world, that we should be holy*** *and without blame before him in love: Having predestinated us unto the adoption of children by Jesus Christ to himself, according to the good pleasure of his will, to the praise of the glory of his grace, wherein he hath made us accepted in the beloved*" (Ephesians 1:2-6). Every believer in Christ is given the distinct privilege of being called a child of God. John said it this way: "***Behold, what manner of love the Father hath bestowed upon us, that we should be called the sons of God: therefore the world knoweth us not, because it knew him not. Beloved, now are we the sons of God, and it doth not yet appear what we shall be: but we know that, when he shall appear, we shall be like him; for we shall see him as he is. And every man that hath this hope in him purifieth himself, even as he is pure***" (I John 3:1-3; see also John 1:10-13). Therefore, walking worthy of your spiritual vocation is living as a child of God.

Paul explained further in Ephesians 4:2 that walking worthy of your spiritual vocation requires four attributes, saying, "***With all lowliness and meekness, with longsuffering, forbearing one another in love.***" The first and third attributes, lowliness and longsuffering, address your attitude. You must view yourself with lowliness (humility), and view others with longsuffering (patience). The second and fourth attributes of meekness and forbearing address your actions based on your attitudes. Because you view yourself in humility, you should be meek (not overbearing with others). Because you have patience, you should be forbearing (willing to suffer due to others' actions). Finally, all of these attributes must be based on biblical love as described in I Corinthians 13:1-8. Paul provided an example of lowliness and longsuffering in Romans 15:1-3 saying, "***We then that are strong ought to bear the infirmities of the weak, and not to please ourselves. Let every one of us please his neighbour for his good to edification. For even Christ pleased not himself; but, as it is written, The reproaches of them that reproached thee fell on me.***"

Paul concluded in Ephesians 4:3 by stating the goal of walking according to your spiritual vocation as a child of God,

The Christian's Walk

saying, "*Endeavouring to keep the unity of the Spirit in the bond of peace.*" Every believer is a child of God by faith in Christ and is indwelt by the Holy Spirit. Therefore you should work to live in loving unity within God's family (Galatians 4:4-6). Romans 14:19 says, "*Let us therefore follow after the things which make for peace, and things wherewith one may edify another.*" Colossians 3:11-15 teaches that there are distinctions of persons in the God's family, saying, "*Where there is neither Greek nor Jew…bond nor free: but Christ is all, and in all. Put on therefore, as the elect of God, holy and beloved, bowels of mercies, kindness, humbleness of mind, meekness, longsuffering; Forbearing one another, and forgiving one another, if any man have a quarrel against any: even as Christ forgave you, so also do ye. And above all these things put on charity, which is the bond of perfectness. And let the peace of God rule in your hearts, to the which also ye are called in one body; and be ye thankful.*" Therefore, you must walk worthy of your spiritual vocation by worshiping and working together with your spiritual brothers and sisters as you humbly and patiently strive for peaceful unity in obedience to God's Word.

Walking Worthy Is a Personal Choice

The New Testament teaches that as a believer, you are to walk worthy, valuing and representing all that you have received through your salvation. Will you commit to walking worthy of God the Father by separating from sin? Will you commit to walking worthy of the Lord Jesus Christ by being fruitful in good works, growing in the knowledge of God the Father, depending on Christ's daily strength, and thanking God regularly for your heavenly inheritance? Will you commit to walking worthy of your spiritual vocation by living in peaceful unity with your spiritual brothers and sisters in God's family? If you are struggling in any of the above areas, why not share your need with God in prayer right now and ask Him to forgive you of any sin, to guide you by His Word, and to encourage you through fellow Christians so that you can begin to walk worthy of God the Father, of the Lord Jesus

Christ, and the vocation to which you have been called as a child of God.

The Christian's Walk

Biblical Principles about Walking Worthy

- ✓ **Matthew 5:48** - As God's children, Christians are called to be perfect like Him.

- ✓ **Titus 2:7-8** - Spiritual leaders are to serve as an example of how to live godly lives.

- ✓ **II Corinthians 6:17-7:1** - God promises Christians His fatherly presence when they separate themselves from sin.

- ✓ **Revelation 5:11-14** - Jesus Christ is worthy to receive all glory from all of creation, both in heaven and on earth.

- ✓ **Matthew 10:37-39** - Being worthy of Jesus Christ requires loving Him above all earthly relationships and processions.

- ✓ **II Thessalonians 1:11-12** - Christians are to live worthy of their spiritual calling and the name of Jesus Christ.

- ✓ **Titus 3:8** - Christians are to be careful to commit good works.

- ✓ **II Corinthians 4:6** - Christians know God the Father better by knowing Jesus Christ better.

- ✓ **Ephesians 6:10-18** - Christians are commanded to depend on Jesus Christ's power as they put on the armor of God.

- ✓ **Matthew 6:19-21** - Christians are to lay up eternal treasures in heaven as an inheritance rather than to be preoccupied with the temporal things of this world.

- ✓ **Philippians 2:1-11** - Christians should follow Jesus Christ's example of humility and sacrifice in order to produce unity and peace.

- ✓ **Romans 12:16-18** - Christians are to work towards peace with others.

- ✓ **Matthew 6:14-15** - God will not forgive Christians who are unforgiving.

- ✓ **I Corinthians 12:12-27** - Christians are to be unified as a body in the local church.

- ✓ _____ - _____

- ✓ _____ - _____

- ✓ _____ - _____

- ✓ _____ - _____

- ✓ _____ - _____

- ✓ _____ - _____

- ✓ _____ - _____

Biblical Investigation about Walking Worthy

✎ Bible Reading: I Thessalonians 2:10-12, Colossians 1:9-14, Ephesians 4:1-4

✎ Bible Memory Verses: I Thessalonians 2:12
12 That ye would walk worthy of God, who hath called you unto his kingdom and glory.

1. Walking worthy is a lifestyle that <u>recognizes</u> and <u>reflects</u> another person's or object's <u>value</u>.

Walking Worthy of God the Father

2. Can you fully understand the greatness and value of God's works? (Job 9:10)
   <u>No</u>
   ☞ What are some examples of God's works that are wonderful but incomprehensible?
   _____
   _____

3. What is God worthy to receive? (Psalm 29:1-2, Revelation 4:8-11)
   <u>Glory, honor, and power</u>
   How should God be worshiped?
   <u>In the beauty of holiness</u>

Walking Worthy

☞ What are some ways that you can give God what He deserves to receive and worship Him according to His holiness?
_____
_____

4. Because Paul valued God the Father, how did Paul behave himself? (I Thessalonians 2:10-12, see also Colossians 1:13, I Peter 2:9-10)
   a   <u>Holily</u>
   b   <u>Justly</u>
   c   <u>Unblameably</u>
   ☞ What are some ways that you can follow Paul's example?
   _____

   What has God done for you that should motivate you to walk worthy of Him?
   d   Called you into his <u>kingdom</u>
   e   Called you into his <u>glory</u>

5. What has God called you to be? (I Peter 1:14-16)
   <u>Holy</u>
   ☞ What does it mean to live holy?
   _____
   _____

Walking Worthy of the Lord Jesus Christ

6. What are the four ways that you can be pleasing to and walk worthy of the Lord Jesus Christ? (Colossians 1:9-12)
   a   <u>Being fruitful in every good work</u>
   b   <u>Increase in the knowledge of God</u>
   c   <u>Be strengthened by Jesus Christ's might</u>
   d   <u>Give thanks unto God the Father for my eternal inheritance</u>

The Christian's Walk

7. Why did Jesus Christ redeem you from your sins? (Titus 2:14)
   <u>So that I may be a pure person, desiring to do good works</u>
   ☞ What are some good works that you know Jesus Christ wants you to do but that you have not been doing faithfully?
   _____
   _____

8. What does God the Father give you when you begin your relationship with Him and Jesus Christ at your salvation? (John 17:3)
   <u>Eternal life</u>

9. What does God the Father give you when you begin your relationship with Him and Jesus Christ at your salvation? (I Peter 1:2-3)
   <u>All that is necessary for life and godliness</u>
   ☞ What are some ways in which you can increase your knowledge of God?
   _____
   _____

10. What do you have the strength to do when you depend on Jesus Christ's strength? (Philippians 4:13; See also II Corinthians 12:7-10)
    <u>All things</u>
    ☞ What are some things that you know God wants you to do but you think you do not have the ability to accomplish?
    _____
    _____

11. How does God's Word describe your spiritual inheritance? (I Peter 1:3-5)
    3 Blessed be the God and Father of our Lord Jesus Christ, which according to his abundant mercy hath begotten us again unto a lively hope by the resurrection of Jesus Christ from the dead,
    4 To an inheritance <u>incorruptible</u>, and <u>undefiled</u>, and that <u>fadeth</u> not away, reserved in <u>heaven</u> for you,
    5 Who are kept by the power of God through faith unto salvation ready to be revealed in the last time.

12. How should you live based on the fact that this world will be dissolved? (II Peter 3:11-13)
    a <u>Holy conversation</u>
    b <u>Godliness</u>

13. Where should you place your affections? (Colossians 3:1-3)
    <u>Above, in heaven</u>
    ☞ How can putting your affections on things above make you thankful?

Walking Worthy
of Your Spiritual Vocation

14. What has God chosen you to be when you believe in the Gospel of Jesus Christ? (Ephesians 1:2-6, I John 3:1-3, John 1:10-13, Galatians 4:4-6)
    <u>His child</u>

The Christian's Walk

15. What are the two attitudes and their matching actions that you must have when you walk worthy of your vocation? (Ephesians 4:1-4)
    a <u>Lowliness / humility</u>   = <u>Meekness / not overbearing</u>
    b <u>Longsuffering / patience</u> = <u>Forbearing / willing to suffer</u>
    What is the overall requirement for you to walk worthy of your vocation?
    <u>Love</u>
    What is the goal of walking worthy of your vocation?
    <u>Unity and peace with my spiritual brothers and sisters</u>

16. Who is your example of treating others with biblical love? (Romans 15:1-3)
    <u>Jesus Christ</u>
    ☞ What are some ways in which you can display biblical love to those around you?
    _____
    _____

17. What is the biblical solution for a lack of peace and unity amongst Christians? (Romans 14:19, Colossians 3:11-15, Ephesians 4:31-32)
    <u>Forgiveness</u>
    What is the example of the above solution?
    <u>How Jesus Christ forgave me</u>
    ☞ Is there anyone that you need to forgive according to the above example?
    Yes / No

Study Guide - Page 39

Walking Worthy
Is a Personal Choice

18. Are there areas of your life that need to change so you can be walk worthy of God the Father, Jesus Christ, and your spiritual vocation? What are those areas, and what changes should you make? Will you ask God for His help to make these changes?

Personal Notes about Walking Worthy

Chapter 3

Walking in Newness of Life
Walking as a New Creature

Romans 6:1-14
1 What shall we say then?
Shall we continue in sin, that grace may abound?
2 God forbid.
How shall we, that are dead to sin,
live any longer therein?
3 Know ye not,
that so many of us as were baptized into Jesus Christ
were baptized into his death?
4 Therefore we are buried with him
by baptism into death:
that like as Christ was raised up from the dead
by the glory of the Father,
even so we also should walk in newness of life.
5 For if we have been planted together
n the likeness of his death,
we shall be also in the likeness of his resurrection:
6 Knowing this, that our old man is crucified with him,
that the body of sin might be destroyed,
that henceforth we should not serve sin.

Galatians 6:14-16

14 But God forbid that I should glory,
save in the cross of our Lord Jesus Christ,
by whom the world is crucified unto me,
and I unto the world.
15 For in Christ Jesus
neither circumcision availeth any thing,
nor uncircumcision,
but a new creature.
16 And as many as walk according to this rule,
peace be on them, and mercy,
and upon the Israel of God.

Chapter 3

Walking in Newness of Life
Walking as a New Creature

Romans 6:1-14
Galatians 6:14-16

Biblical Instruction about Walking in Newness of Life

In Romans 6:1-14, the apostle Paul revealed the practical significance of identifying with Christ's death, burial, and resurrection for salvation while answering the logical question, *"Shall we continue in sin, that grace may abound?"* Paul had previously explained to the believers in Rome that the salvation provided by God through Christ is based on God's grace, saying in part, *"Therefore being justified by faith, we have peace with God through our Lord Jesus Christ: By whom also we have access by faith into this grace wherein we stand, and rejoice in hope of the glory of God"* (Romans 5:1-2). In addition, he assured the believers that God's grace was more than sufficient to forgive all their sins, saying, *"Moreover the law entered, that the offense might abound. But where sin abounded, grace did much more abound: That as sin hath reigned unto death, even so might grace reign through righteousness unto eternal life by Jesus Christ our Lord"* (Romans 5:20-21). But, now that the believers knew of God's abundant grace to forgive sin, Paul needed to confront the human temptation to abuse such grace by sinning more frequently and thereby experiencing God's grace more regularly. Paul's answer to this human logic was an emphatic, *"God forbid. How shall we, that are dead to sin, live any longer*

Walking in Newness of Life

therein?" (Romans 6:2). He later added, "*we also should walk in newness of life*" (Romans 6:4). *Walking in newness of life is a lifestyle of living free from the authority of sin with the purpose of glorifying God by obeying the authority of righteousness.*

Walking in Newness of Life Requires Identifying with Jesus Christ's Death, Burial, and Resurrection

After Paul made it clear that believers should not use God's grace as an excuse to sin, he explained that all believers, because of their identification with Christ's death, burial, and resurrection, have been freed from sin's authority. He said, "*Know ye not, that so many of us as were baptized into Jesus Christ were baptized into his death? Therefore we are buried with him by baptism into death: that like as Christ was raised up from the dead by the glory of the Father, even so we also should walk in newness of life*" (Romans 6:3-4). When you placed your faith in Christ as your personal Savior, you were spiritually baptized, or placed into, Christ (Galatians 3:26-27). Therefore, in God the Father's eyes, when Jesus died on the cross, you died with Him. When He was buried in the tomb, you were buried with him. And when He rose from the dead on the third day, you rose with Him (Colossians 2:10-15). So, "*like as Christ was raised up from the dead by the glory of the Father, even so we also should walk in newness of life*" (Romans 6:4). As II Corinthians 5:17 says, "*Therefore if any man be in Christ, he is a new creature: old things are passed away; behold, all things are become new.*" In Galatians 6:14-16, Paul declared, "*But God forbid that I should glory, save in the cross of our Lord Jesus Christ, by whom the world is crucified unto me, and I unto the world. For in Christ Jesus neither circumcision availeth any thing, nor uncircumcision, but a new creature. And as many as walk according to this rule, peace be on them, and mercy, and upon the Israel of God.*" God the Father, in His abundant grace, saved you from your sin and gave you eternal life in which you can enjoy His peace and mercy both here on earth and in heaven for all eternity.

The Christian's Walk

Walking in Newness of Life Rejects the Authority of Sin

In Romans 6:6-7, Paul explained "*that our old man is crucified with him, that the body of sin might be destroyed, that henceforth we should not serve sin. For he that is dead is freed from sin.*" When you trusted in Christ as your personal Savior, your old man, or your natural tendency to obey temptation that then results in sin, was crucified with Christ (James 1:13-15). Galatians 5:24 says, "*And they that are Christ's have crucified the flesh with the affections and lusts.*" Your crucifixion in Christ has liberated you from sin's authority, allowing you to choose to walk in a new lifestyle. However, you must choose to "*Stand fast therefore in the liberty wherewith Christ hath made us free, and be not entangled again with the yoke of bondage*" (Galatians 5:1). "*For, brethren, ye have been called unto liberty; only use not liberty for an occasion to the flesh, but by love serve one another*" (Galatians 5:13).

In Ephesians 4:22-24, Paul, after revealing the wickedness of the old man, added, "*But ye have not so learned Christ; If so be that ye have heard him, and have been taught by him, as the truth is in Jesus: That ye put off concerning the former conversation the old man, which is corrupt according to the deceitful lusts; And be renewed in the spirit of your mind; And that ye put on the new man, which after God is created in righteousness and true holiness.*" Your old way of living according to sin's authority led you to need salvation through Christ's crucifixion. Therefore, it is logical that you would reject sin's authority and accept the authority of Christ's righteousness in your new life. James 4:6-8 adds, "*But he giveth more grace. Wherefore he saith, God resisteth the proud, but giveth grace unto the humble. Submit yourselves therefore to God. Resist the devil, and he will flee from you. Draw nigh to God, and he will draw nigh to you. Cleanse your hands, ye sinners; and purify your hearts, ye double-minded.*" God's grace is sufficient to not only save your from your past sins but also to protect you from your present and future sins, but you must humbly and purposefully seek God's help in your time of temptation.

Walking in Newness of Life

Walking in Newness of Life Recognizes the Authority of Righteousness

It is wonderful news that you have been liberated from the authority of sin, but there is even more excellent news. Because you died spiritually with Christ on the cross, you rose again with Him so that you might "*also live with him*" (Romans 6:8). However, living with Christ does not start when you arrive in heaven. As studied in chapter one, you can live with Christ today.

In Romans 6:9-10, Paul explained further, saying, "***Knowing that Christ being raised from the dead dieth no more; death hath no more dominion over him. For in that he died, he died unto sin once: but in that he liveth, he liveth unto God.***" Just as Christ died for man's sins and rose again by God's power to live for God's glory, you must choose to live for God in appreciation of everything His grace has given you. For this reason, Paul added, "***Likewise reckon ye also yourselves to be dead indeed unto sin, but alive unto God through Jesus Christ our Lord. Let not sin therefore reign in your mortal body, that ye should obey it in the lusts thereof. Neither yield ye your members as instruments of unrighteousness unto sin: but yield yourselves unto God, as those that are alive from the dead, and your members as instruments of righteousness unto God. For sin shall not have dominion over you: for ye are not under the law, but under grace***" (Romans 6:11-14). In each day of your new life in Christ, you must "*reckon*," or believe as a fact from God, that you have been freed from the authority of sin and can live with Christ under the authority of God's righteousness. The apostle John revealed that "***All unrighteousness is sin***" (I John 5:17; see also I John 3:4). Therefore, you cannot enjoy walking in the newness of life with Christ while living in sin. You must choose to live a resurrected life that imitates Christ's righteousness.

Walking in Newness of Life Is a Personal Choice

Romans 6:1-14 teaches that by identifying with Christ's death, burial, and resurrection for your salvation, you have been given a new life of righteousness with Christ. Will you commit to

The Christian's Walk

accepting God's gracious forgiveness of your past sins? Will you commit to rejecting future sins, recognizing that temptation has no authority over you? Will you commit to living with Christ, in resurrection power, to do what God calls righteous? If you are struggling in any of the above areas, why not share your need with God in prayer right now and ask Him to forgive you of any sin, to guide you by His Word, and to encourage you through fellow Christians so that you can begin to walk in newness of life.

Biblical Principles about Walking in Newness of Life

- ✓ **Romans 6:15-22** - Christians are not to serve sin because they are God's servants.

- ✓ **II Corinthians 5:14-17** - Christians are to live for Jesus Christ because of His great love for them.

- ✓ **II Corinthians 4:10-11** - Christians are to consider themselves dead to this world so that Jesus Christ can live through them.

- ✓ **I Peter 4:1-3** - Christians are to live according to God's will rather than their own lusts.

- ✓ **II Timothy 2:19-22** - Christians are to separate from sin because they identify with the name of Jesus Christ.

- ✓ **I Corinthians 6:19-20** - Christians have been bought by the sacrifice of Jesus Christ and are to live for the glory of God.

- ✓ **Romans 12:1-2** - Christians are to present themselves as holy, living sacrifices to God.

- ✓ **Colossians 3:1-10** - Christians are to put away their old man and put on the new man, which is in the image of Jesus Christ.

- ✓ **II Corinthians 13:4** - Christians are to live according to God's resurrection power.

Walking in Newness of Life

- ✓ **I Peter 2:21-25** - Jesus Christ, being without sin, sacrificed himself for man's sin so that each Christian can live in righteousness.

- ✓ _____ - _____

- ✓ _____ - _____

- ✓ _____ - _____

- ✓ _____ - _____

- ✓ _____ - _____

- ✓ _____ - _____

- ✓ _____ - _____

- ✓ _____ - _____

- ✓ _____ - _____

- ✓ _____ - _____

The Christian's Walk

Biblical Investigation about Walking in Newness of Life

✎ Bible Reading: Romans 6:1-14, Galatians 6:14-16
☞ Bible Memory: Romans 6:3-4

> **3 Know ye not, that so many of us as were baptized into Jesus Christ were baptized into his death?**
> **4 Therefore we are buried with him by baptism into death: that like as Christ was raised up from the dead by the glory of the Father, even so we also should walk in newness of life.**

1. Walking in newness of life is a lifestyle of living free from the <u>authority</u> of <u>sin</u> with the purpose of <u>glorifying</u> God by <u>obeying</u> the <u>authority</u> of <u>righteousness</u>.

2. What is Paul's answer to the question, "Shall we continue in sin, that grace may abound?" (Romans 6:1)
   <u>God forbid. How shall we, that are dead to sin, live any longer therein?</u>

3. How do you have access to God's grace that has justified you and given you peace with God? (Romans 5:1-2)
   <u>By faith in Jesus Christ for salvation</u>

4. What word describes the amount of God's grace to cover all of your sins? (Romans 5:20-21)
   <u>Abound</u>

Walking in Newness of Life
Requires Identifying with Jesus Christ's
Death, Burial, and Resurrection

5. What should be the result of identifying with Jesus Christ's death, burial, and resurrection? (Romans 6:3-4, Galatians 3:26-27, Colossians 2:10-15)
   <u>Walking in newness of life</u>
   ☞ What are some ways that a believer's lifestyle should be different from an unbeliever's?
   _____
   _____

6. What does God make you when you are in Jesus Christ? (II Corinthians 5:17)
   <u>A new creature</u>
   How much of your life has been made new?
   <u>All of it ("all things")</u>
   ☞ What are a few things you are glad God has made new in your life?
   _____
   _____

7. What can you enjoy when you walk as a new creature? (Galatians 6:14-16)
   a <u>Peace</u>
   b <u>Mercy</u>

Walking in Newness of Life
Rejects the Authority of Sin

8. Why are you no longer required to listen to the authority of sin? (Romans 6:6-7)
   Because I died with Jesus Christ and am dead to sin
   What part of you was crucified with Jesus Christ?
   My old man

9. Does God tempt you with sin? (James 1:13-15)
   No
   Whose lusts tempt you to sin?
   My own
   ☞ What are some areas of your life in which you are frequently tempted?

   What is the result of sin?
   Death = separation from God

10. What must you consider crucified with Jesus Christ? (Galatians 5:24)
    My flesh

11. What must you choose to do with the liberty that Jesus Christ has given you? (Galatians 5:1, 13)
    Stand fast in it
    How should you not use your liberty?
    For the flesh
    How should you use your liberty
    Serve others in love

Walking in Newness of Life

☞ What are some ways that you can use your liberty for good?
_____
_____

12. What two words describe how God has created your new man? (Ephesians 4:22-24)
    a Righteousness
    b True Holiness

13. What two things must you humbly do to experience God's grace when you are tempted? (James 4:6-8)
    a Submit to God - Draw nigh to God
    b Resist the Devil

Walking in Newness of Life
Recognizes the Authority of Righteousness

14. With Whom do you have the privilege of living throughout your new life? (Romans 6:8-10)
    Jesus Christ
    ☞ How might the reality that Jesus Christ is living with you affect your choices about sin?
    _____
    _____

    For Whom should you live in your new life?
    God the Father
    ☞ How might the reality that you are to live for God the Father affect your choices about sin?
    _____
    _____
    _____

The Christian's Walk

15. What must you do if you are going to be able to reject sins' authority? (Romans 6:11-14)

    11 Likewise <u>reckon</u> ye also yourselves to be <u>dead</u> indeed unto <u>sin</u>, but <u>alive</u> unto <u>God</u> through Jesus Christ our Lord.
    12 Let not sin therefore <u>reign</u> in your mortal <u>body</u>, that ye should <u>obey</u> it in the <u>lusts</u> thereof.
    13 Neither <u>yield</u> ye your <u>members</u> as instruments of unrighteousness unto <u>sin</u>: but <u>yield</u> yourselves unto <u>God</u>, as those that are alive from the dead, and your <u>members</u> as instruments of <u>righteousness</u> unto God.
    14 For <u>sin</u> shall not have <u>dominion</u> over you: for ye are not under the law, but under <u>grace</u>.

16. What is sin? (I John 5:17; see also I John 3:4)
    <u>Unrighteousness</u>
    Can sin and righteousness work together?
    Yes / No
    ☞ What are some areas of your life that you know you must choose to reject sin and obey righteousness?
    _____
    _____

Walking in Newness of Life
Is a Personal Choice

17. Are there areas of your life that should change so you can be walk in newness of life? What are those areas, and what changes should you make? Will you ask God for His help to make these changes?

_____
_____
_____
_____
_____
_____
_____
_____
_____
_____
_____
_____
_____
_____
_____
_____
_____
_____
_____
_____
_____
_____
_____

Personal Notes about Walking in Newness of Life

Chapter 4

Walking in Good Works

Ephesians 2:8-10
8 For by grace are ye saved through faith;
and that not of yourselves: it is the gift of God:
9 Not of works, lest any man should boast.
10 For we are his workmanship,
created in Christ Jesus unto good works,
which God hath before ordained
hat we should walk in them.

Chapter 4

Walking in Good Works

Ephesians 2:8-10

A Biblical Instruction about Walking in Good Works

In Ephesians 2:8-9, the apostle Paul revealed one of the most fundamental truths about biblical salvation, saying, ***"For by grace are ye saved through faith; and that not of yourselves: it is the gift of God: Not of works, lest any man should boast."*** Because of man's sin nature, he cannot earn salvation on his own. Instead, he must place his faith in God's gracious gift found in Christ's sacrifice on the cross (I Peter 3:18). Romans 3:20 says, ***"Therefore by the deeds of the law there shall no flesh be justified in his sight: for by the law is the knowledge of sin."*** Romans 3:28 adds, ***"Therefore we conclude that a man is justified by faith without the deeds of the law."*** Make no mistake, salvation is either by God's grace, or it is by man's works; it cannot be both (Romans 11:6). The Bible is clear that God provides salvation through Christ as a free gift that must be accepted by faith and that no man, woman, or child can ever do enough good works to earn heaven.

After establishing the fundamental truth that man's salvation is a gift of grace, given by God and received through faith alone, Paul continued in Ephesians 2:10, saying, ***"For we are his workmanship, created in Christ Jesus unto good works, which God hath before ordained that we should walk in them."*** At the moment of your salvation, God made you ***"a new creature: old things are passed away; behold, all things are become new"*** (II

Walking in Good Works

Corinthians 5:17). God the Father's plans for your new life did not end at forgiving your past sins and giving you eternal life in the future. He has also taken special care to re-create you with an ability that you did not possess before. In the past, you could not do any truly good works. It may have appeared to others that you had been kind, forgiving, hardworking, etc., but God's holy eyes could still see your sinfulness. "***As it is written, There is none righteous, no, not one: There is none that understandeth, there is none that seeketh after God. They are all gone out of the way, they are together become unprofitable; there is none that doeth good, no, not one***" (Romans 3:10-12). Because you could not be holy like Him, your best works were never considered good in God's eyes. However, God changed you by re-creating you into a brand new person at your salvation. Although you could never have earned salvation through good works, you have been re-created in Christ by God the Father for the purpose of doing good works. Jesus said, "***Let your light so shine before men, that they may see your good works, and glorify your Father which is in heaven***" (Matthew 5:16). *Walking in good works is a lifestyle of choosing to do that which God considers to be good in such a way that He receives the glory.*

Walking in Good Works Fulfills Your God-Given Purpose

Ephesians 2:10 reveals that God the Father, the perfect Creator, carefully re-created you to do good works, saying, "***For we are his workmanship, created in Christ Jesus unto good works, which God hath before ordained that we should walk in them.***" Although before your salvation you may have doubted your life's purpose, after your salvation, God has made your purpose very clear: you are to do good works. More specifically, Romans 8:29 says, "***For whom he did foreknow, he also did predestinate to be conformed to the image of his Son.***" God has saved you from your sins so that you can begin to live as Jesus lived—full of good works.

The Christian's Walk

In Philippians 1:6, the Bible reveals that at your salvation, God began to do a work in your life that He will continue to fulfill until you reach heaven, saying, "*He which hath begun a good work in you will perform it until the day of Jesus Christ.*" However, God will not force you to do what you do not want to do, just like He did not force you to accept His salvation. Instead, Philippians 2:13 says that He will work within your desires, encouraging you to want what He knows is best for you, when it says, "*For it is God which worketh in you both to will and to do of his good pleasure.*" Hebrews 13:20-21 explains further, saying, "*Now the God of peace, that brought again from the dead our Lord Jesus, that great shepherd of the sheep, through the blood of the everlasting covenant, make you perfect in every good work to do his will, working in you that which is wellpleasing in his sight, through Jesus Christ; to whom be glory for ever and ever. Amen.*"

The changes that must be made in your life cannot be made in your own power. Before you were saved you lived in your own power, which resulted in sin and sorrow. If you attempt to live your new life according to your own power, it will also bring sin and sorrow. However, the grace that saved you from your sins is the same grace God offers to help you live your new life in Christ and to produce good works instead of evil works. II Corinthians 9:8 promises that "*God is able to make all grace abound toward you; that ye, always having all sufficiency in all things, may abound to every good work.*" God's grace is abundant. It is more than enough to help you not only do a few good deeds from time to time but to "*abound*" in "*every good work*" that God desires for you to do (II Corinthians 9:8).

But there is more; God has given you two spiritual resources to guide and encourage you to do good works. First, in II Timothy 3:16-17, the Bible says, "*All scripture is given by inspiration of God, and is profitable for doctrine, for reproof, for correction, for instruction in righteousness: that the man of God may be perfect, throughly furnished unto all good works.*" God has

Walking in Good Works

provided you with an instruction manual called the Bible that teaches you how to do good works after your salvation. As you read it personally and hear it taught publically with your heart open to obey it, you can be assured that God's grace will prepare and empower you to do all the good works He has planned for each and every day of your life. Second, in Hebrews 10:24-25 the Bible says, "*And let us consider one another to provoke unto love and to good works: Not forsaking the assembling of ourselves together, as the manner of some is; but exhorting one another: and so much the more, as ye see the day approaching.*" God has given you a group of people in your local church to encourage you to obey God's Word. Regularly attending your local church allows you to be encouraged by and to encourage other believers to obey God's Word so that you can all fulfill good works before the lost world around you (Galatians 6:10).

Walking in Good Works Allows Jesus Christ to Work through Your Daily Activities

Ephesians 2:10 declares that at the moment of your salvation, you were "*created in Christ Jesus unto good works.*" Such a statement should not surprise you. As mentioned in chapter three, your old man has been crucified with Christ, and you have risen again with resurrection power (Romans 6:1-13). Titus 2:11-14 explains further, saying, "*For the grace of God that bringeth salvation hath appeared to all men, teaching us that, denying ungodliness and worldly lusts, we should live soberly, righteously, and godly, in this present world; Looking for that blessed hope, and the glorious appearing of the great God and our Saviour Jesus Christ; Who gave himself for us, that he might redeem us from all iniquity, and purify unto himself a peculiar people, zealous of good works.*" Jesus graciously sacrificed Himself to save you so that He could change your entire life from the inside out. Whereas your old life can be described as "*foolish, disobedient, deceived, serving divers lusts and pleasures, living in malice and envy, hateful, and hating one another*," you should now "*be careful to maintain good works*" as you "*speak evil of no man…but gentle, shewing all meekness unto all men.*" (Titus 3:1-8). Please understand, Jesus does not force you to do good works that glorify God. Rather, He desires that you would be "*zealous*" to do good works out of appreciation for your salvation (Titus 2:14; see also Luke 7:36-50).

Just as Jesus's earthly life and ministry were full of good works, so you must allow Him to live through you to produce good works in each of your daily activities (Galatians 2:20). Jesus said in John 14:12, "*Verily, verily, I say unto you, He that believeth on me, the works that I do shall he do also; and greater works than these shall he do; because I go unto my Father.*" Today, in Jesus's absence, you represent His works as you live according to His example. Because God has given you "*victory through our Lord Jesus Christ*" over the power of sin-filled, evil works, you are to be "*stedfast, unmoveable, always abounding in the work of the Lord, forasmuch as ye know that your labour is not in vain in the Lord*" (I Corinthians 15:57-58).

Walking in Good Works Is a Personal Choice

The New Testament's teaching on walking in good works is very clear. You have been saved from your old sinful works by God's grace, and He has re-created you in Christ for the purpose of doing good works. However, the choice to do good works is yours alone. Have you taken time to consider how your life should change because of God's gracious salvation? Are you regularly reflecting on and attempting to follow Christ's example of good works? Are you relying on God's grace to guide and empower you to replace your sinful habits with new God-honoring habits? Are you regularly learning from God's Word so that you know what good works He wants you to perform? Are you regularly gathering with fellow believers to be encouraged and to encourage them to obey God's Word by doing good works? What areas of your life have you not been fulfilling good works? What changes must you make to be abounding in good works for God's glory?

The Christian's Walk

Biblical Principles about Walking in Good Works

- ✓ **Romans 3:10-25** - A Christian is saved by God's grace alone–not by his own good works.

- ✓ **I Peter 2:11-12** - A Christian's good works should produce glory for God.

- ✓ **I Timothy 5:24-25** - A Christian's good works may be hidden for a time or revealed to others.

- ✓ **II Timothy 2:19-21** - Christians are to remove dishonorable works of iniquity from their lives so that they are clean instruments ready to do good works.

- ✓ **James 2:14-26** - A Christian's good works are evidence of His faith in Jesus Christ as His personal Savior.

- ✓ **Colossians 1:9-12** - Christians are to be fruitful in good works.

- ✓ **II Thessalonians 2:16-17** - God the Father establishes Christians in good works.

- ✓ **Titus 2:7-8** - The spiritual leaders within the local church are to be examples of doing good works.

- ✓ _____ - _____

- ✓ _____ - _____

Walking in Good Works

- ✓ _____ - _____
- ✓ _____ - _____
- ✓ _____ - _____
- ✓ _____ - _____
- ✓ _____ - _____
- ✓ _____ - _____
- ✓ _____ - _____
- ✓ _____ - _____
- ✓ _____ - _____
- ✓ _____ - _____
- ✓ _____ - _____
- ✓ _____ - _____

Biblical Investigation about Walking in Good Works

✎ Bible Reading: Ephesians 2:8-10
✎ Bible Memory Verse: Ephesians 2:10
10 For we are his workmanship, created in Christ Jesus unto good works, which God hath before ordained that we should walk in them.

1. Walking in good works is a lifestyle of <u>choosing</u> to do that which <u>God</u> considers to be <u>good</u> in such a way that He receives the <u>glory</u>.

2. How have you been saved? (Ephesians 2:8-10, Romans 3:20, 28, 11:6)
   <u>By faith in God's gift of grace</u>
   Can you work your way to heaven?
   Yes / <u>No</u>
   ☞ What are some good works people do in order to try to earn heaven?
   _____

   What did God do to you the moment you were saved?
   <u>Re-created me in Christ Jesus</u>
   In what has God ordained that you should walk after your salvation?
   <u>Good works</u>

3. Why did Jesus Christ suffer to provide you salvation? (I Peter 3:18)
   <u>To bring me to God</u>

Walking in Good Works

4. What did God make you at the moment of your salvation? (II Corinthians 5:17)
   <u>A new creature</u>
   What is true about your old life following your salvation?
   <u>It has passed away</u>
   ☞ What are some things from your old life that you are thankful God has dealt with?

   _____

5. Could you do good before your salvation? (Romans 3:10-12)
   Yes / No

6. Who should receive glory from your good works? (Matthew 5:16).
   <u>My heavenly Father</u>
   ☞ What are some ways that your good works can glorify God?

   _____

Walking in Good Works
Fulfills Your God-Given Purpose

7. After salvation, Whose workmanship are you? (Ephesians 2:10)
   <u>God's</u>
   ☞ What does it mean that you are God's workmanship?

   _____

   What has God created you to do?
   <u>Good works</u>
   ☞ What are some good works that you know God wants you to do regularly?

   _____

The Christian's Walk

8. In Whose image has God predestined you to look like? (Romans 8:29)
   <u>Jesus Christ's</u>
   ☞ What does it mean to be conformed to His image?
   _____
   _____

9. What has God begun in you? (Philippians 1:6)
   <u>A good work</u>
   How long will God work in you to accomplish what He has begun?
   <u>Until the coming of Jesus Christ</u>

10. What is God working in you to encourage you to do? (Philippians 2:13)
    13 For it is God which worketh in you both to <u>will</u> and to <u>do</u> of his <u>good pleasure</u>.

11. In what does God want to make you perfect? (Hebrews 13:20-21)
    <u>In every good work</u>
    ☞ What are some individual good works that God is preparing you to do?
    _____
    _____

12. What does God make abound toward you? (II Corinthians 9:8)
    <u>All grace</u>
    In what does God want to make you sufficient?
    <u>All things</u>
    In what does He want to make you abound?
    <u>Every good work</u>

Walking in Good Works

13. Who gave you the Word of God? (II Timothy 3:16-17)
    <u>God</u>
    For what are the four things is the Word of God profitable?
    a <u>Doctrine</u>
    b <u>Reproof</u>
    c <u>Correction</u>
    d <u>Instruction in righteousness</u>
    What does the Word of God furnish you to do?
    <u>Good works</u>
    ☞ What good works have you recently learned from the Bible that God desires for you?

    _____

14. What should you provoke other believers to do? (Hebrews 10:24-25)
    a <u>Love</u>
    b <u>Good works</u>
    What must you not do?
    <u>Forsake assembling with other believers</u>
    ☞ What are your local church's service times?

    _____

    ☞ Are you committed to attend each of those services?
    Yes / No
    What should you do when you are assembled with other believers?
    <u>Exhort them</u>

15. For whom should you do good works? (Galatians 6:10)
    <u>All men</u>
    For whom should you be especially careful to do good works?
    <u>Those in the household of faith</u>

The Christian's Walk

Walking in Good Works
Allows Jesus Christ to Work through Your Daily Activities

16. In Whom were you created so that you can do good works? (Ephesians 2:10, Romans 6:1-13)
    Jesus Christ

17. What does the grace of salvation teach you after you are saved? (Titus 2:11-14)
    11 For the __grace__ of God that bringeth __salvation__ hath appeared to all men,
    12 __teaching__ us that __denying__ __ungodliness__ and __worldly__ lusts we should __live__ __soberly__, __righteously__, and __godly__, in this present world;
    13 __looking for__ that blessed __hope__, and the glorious __appearing__ of the great God and our Saviour Jesus Christ;
    Why did Jesus Christ give Himself to save you?
    14 who gave himself for us, that he might __redeem__ us from all __iniquity__, and __purify__ unto himself a __peculiar__ people, __zealous__ of good __works__.
    ☞ What does it mean to be zealous about good works?
    _____
    _____

18. What are some descriptions of your life before your salvation? (Titus 3:1-8)
    a Foolish
    b Disobedient
    c Deceived
    d Serving diverse lusts and pleasures
    e Living in malice and envy
    f Hateful
    g Hating one another

Walking in Good Works

What changed your life?
<u>The loving kindness of God</u>
How was God's mercy of salvation shed on you?
<u>Abundantly</u>
What should you be careful to maintain if you have received God's salvation?
<u>Good works</u>

19. What will determine the amount of love you have for God? (Luke 7:36-50)
    <u>How much I recognize the greatness of His forgiveness</u>
    ☞ What are some sins for which you have received God's forgiveness?

    ☞ How much appreciation do you believe God deserves due to His forgiveness for the above sins?

20. Who should live through your life after your salvation? (Galatians 2:20, II Corinthians 5:14-15)
    <u>Jesus Christ</u>
    Why should you allow Him to live through your life?
    <u>Because He loved me and gave Himself for me</u>

21. What does Jesus Christ promise you that you will be able to do if you believe in Him? (John 14:12)
    <u>Greater works than He had done</u>
    ☞ What are some works that you need Jesus Christ's help to do?

22. Who has given you victory over sin and death? (I Corinthians 15:57-58)
    <u>God the Father through Jesus Christ</u>
    Because you have victory over sin and death, how should you live?
    a <u>Steadfast</u>
    b <u>Unmoveable</u>
    c <u>Always abounding in the work of the Lord</u>
    Are your good works ever done in vain before the Lord?
    Yes / No

Walking in Good Works Is a Personal Choice

23. Are there areas of your life that should be changed so you can be walking in good works? What are those areas, and what changes should you make? Will you ask God for His help to make these changes?

    _____
    _____
    _____
    _____
    _____
    _____
    _____
    _____
    _____
    _____
    _____
    _____
    _____
    _____

Personal Notes about Walking in Good Works

Walking in Good Works

Chapter 5

Walking in the Light
Walking in Love
Walking in Truth
Walking Circumspectly
Walking after Commandments

John 8:12
12 Then spake Jesus again unto them, saying,
I am the light of the world:
he that followeth me shall not walk in darkness,
but shall have the light of life.

John 12:35-47
35 Then Jesus said unto them,
Yet a little while is the light with you.
Walk while ye have the light,
lest darkness come upon you:
for he that walketh in darkness
knoweth not whither he goeth.
36 While ye have light, believe in the light,
that ye may be the children of light...

Romans 13:12-14
12 The night is far spent, the day is at hand:
et us therefore cast off the works of darkness,
and let us put on the armour of light.
13 Let us walk honestly, as in the day;
not in rioting and drunkenness,
not in chambering and wantonness,
not in strife and envying.

Romans 14:1-23

15 But if thy brother be grieved with thy meat,
now walkest thou not charitably.
Destroy not him with thy meat,
for whom Christ died.

II Corinthians 4:1-2

1 Therefore seeing we have this ministry,
as we have received mercy, we faint not;
2 But have renounced the hidden things of dishonesty,
not walking in craftiness,
nor handling the word of God deceitfully;
but by manifestation of the truth
commending ourselves to every man's conscience
in the sight of God.

Ephesians 5:1-16

1 Be ye therefore followers of God,
as dear children;
2 And walk in love,
as Christ also hath loved us,
and hath given himself for us an offering and a sacrifice
to God for a sweetsmelling savour.
8 For ye were sometimes darkness,
but now are ye light in the Lord:
walk as children of light:
14 Wherefore he saith,
Awake thou that sleepest,
and arise from the dead,
and Christ shall give thee light.
15 See then that ye walk circumspectly,
not as fools, but as wise,
16 Redeeming the time, because the days are evil.

I John 1:5-9

5 This then is the message which we have heard of him,
and declare unto you, that God is light,
and in him is no darkness at all.
6 If we say that we have fellowship with him,
and walk in darkness, we lie, and do not the truth:
7 But if we walk in the light, as he is in the light,
we have fellowship one with another,
and the blood of Jesus Christ his Son
cleanseth us from all sin.

I John 2:7-11

11 But he that hateth his brother is in darkness, and
walketh in darkness, and knoweth not whither he goeth,
because that darkness hath blinded his eyes.

II John 1:4-6

4 I rejoiced greatly
that I found of thy children walking in truth,
as we have received a commandment from the Father.
5 And now I beseech thee, lady,
not as though I wrote a new commandment unto thee,
but that which we had from the beginning,
that we love one another.
6 And this is love, that we walk after his
commandments.
This is the commandment,
That, as ye have heard from the beginning,
ye should walk in it.

III John 1:3-6

3 For I rejoiced greatly, when the brethren came
and testified of the truth that is in thee,
even as thou walkest in the truth.
4 I have no greater joy
than to hear that my children walk in truth.
5 Beloved, thou doest faithfully
whatsoever thou doest to the brethren, and to strangers;
6 Which have borne witness of thy charity...

Chapter 5

Walking in the Light
Walking in Love
Walking in Truth
Walking Circumspectly
Walking after Commandments

John 8:12, 12:35-47
Romans 13:12-14, 14:1-23
II Corinthians 4:1-2
Ephesians 5:1-16
I John 1:5-9, 2:7-11
II John 1:4-6
III John 1:3-6

Biblical Instruction about Walking in the Light

In John 8:12, while standing in front of a crowd, Jesus boldly declared, *"I am the light of the world: he that followeth me shall not walk in darkness, but shall have the light of life."* Jesus used a simple illustration to teach a significant spiritual truth: His spiritual light represents His holy righteousness, which produces spiritual life, while spiritual darkness represents man's sinful unrighteousness, which produces spiritual death. Having come as the light of the world, Jesus offered His light to all those who would follow Him so that He might save them from their darkness (John 12:46). A short time later, once again, while in front of a crowd, Jesus added, *"Yet a little while is the light with you. Walk*

Walking in the Light

while ye have the light, lest darkness come upon you: for he that walketh in darkness knoweth not whither he goeth. While ye have light, believe in the light, that ye may be the children of light" (John 12:35-36). Therefore, at the moment you believed in Jesus to be your personal Savior, you were not only made a child of God but were also given His light of righteousness and were made a child of light (John 1:12). Each child of light should strive to walk in God's light throughout each of their day-to-day activities.

In the New Testament, being an obedient child of God that walks in His light always requires following Christ's example of doing that which is righteous. However, like the two Great Commandments, walking in the light requires a proper relationship both with God the Father and with others (Matthew 22:38-40). Furthermore, the apostle John connects walking in the light with walking in truth and walking in love. First, in II John 1:4, he stated that walking in truth is obedience to God the Father's commandment, saying, "*I rejoiced greatly that I found of thy children walking in truth, as we have received a commandment from the Father.*" Then he explained that God's commandment is to love others, saying, "*not as though I wrote a new commandment unto thee, but that which we had from the beginning, that we love one another. And this is love, that we walk after his commandments. This is the commandment, That, as ye have heard from the beginning, ye should walk in it*" (II John 1:5-6). Finally, in I John 2:9-11, he declares, "*He that saith he is in the light, and hateth his brother, is in darkness even until now. He that loveth his brother abideth in the light, and there is none occasion of stumbling in him. But he that hateth his brother is in darkness, and walketh in darkness, and knoweth not whither he goeth, because that darkness hath blinded his eyes.*" *Walking in the light is a lifestyle of living in a agreement with Jesus Christ's righteousness by maintaining a proper relationship with God the Father by walking in His truth and having a proper relationship with others by walking in love.*

The Christian's Walk

Walking in the Light through Fellowship with God the Father

While Jesus was on earth, He was the spiritual light, sent from heaven by God the Father, to illuminate this sin-darkened world (John 1:1-13, 9:5). However, the Bible records that although Jesus came to share His light with the whole world, *"men loved darkness rather than light, because their deeds were evil. For every one that doeth evil hateth the light, neither cometh to the light, lest his deeds should be reproved. But he that doeth truth cometh to the light, that his deeds may be made manifest, that they are wrought in God"* (John 3:16-21). Those who desire to have fellowship with God the Father must live in the light of Christ by allowing their deeds to be reproved and cleansed by His truth. I John 1:5-7 says, *"This then is the message which we have heard of him, and declare unto you, that God is light, and in him is no darkness at all. If we say that we have fellowship with him and walk in darkness, we lie, and do not the truth: But if we walk in the light, as he is in the light, we have fellowship one with another, and the blood of Jesus Christ his Son cleanseth us from all sin."* In order to enjoy daily fellowship with God the Father, you must be willing to allow the light of His truth to penetrate into your daily activities for the purpose of revealing and then removing those things God calls sin.

In II Corinthians 4:1-2, Paul, while describing his ministry for God and to others, said, *"Therefore seeing we have this ministry, as we have received mercy, we faint not; But have renounced the hidden things of dishonesty, not walking in craftiness, nor handling the word of God deceitfully; but by manifestation of the truth commending ourselves to every man's conscience in the sight of God."* Paul had committed to not be involved in any teaching or action that did not align with God's truth. He challenged the believers in Rome to do the same: *"The night is far spent, the day is at hand: let us therefore cast off the works of darkness, and let us put on the armour of light. Let us walk honestly, as in the day; not in rioting and drunkenness, not in chambering and wantonness, not in strife and envying. But put ye on the Lord Jesus Christ, and make not provision for the flesh, to fulfil the lusts thereof*" (Romans 12:12-14). Living according to the world's philosophy and one's fleshly desires leads away from the light of God's Word and into sin.

Because of the danger of sin and its darkness, Paul said to the believers in Corinth, "***Be ye not unequally yoked together with unbelievers: for what fellowship hath righteousness with unrighteousness? and what communion hath light with darkness? And what concord hath Christ with Belial? or what part hath he that believeth with an infidel? And what agreement hath the temple of God with idols? for ye are the temple of the living God; as God hath said, I will dwell in them, and walk in them; and I will be their God, and they shall be my people. Wherefore come out from among them, and be ye separate, saith the Lord, and touch not the unclean thing; and I will receive you; and I will receive you, and will be a Father unto you, and ye shall be my sons and daughters, saith the Lord Almighty***" (II Corinthians 6:14-18). God the Father knows how precious earthly relationships are to you. But He also knows how damaging they can be if those relationships lead you into the darkness of unrighteousness. Therefore, He promises that if you separate yourself from those relationships that will lead you into sin, He will reward you with a closer relationship with Himself as your heavenly Daddy. God the Father does not want you to be without relationships but rather desires for you to have the right kind of relationships that will be guided by His righteous light.

When you trusted in Christ as your personal Saviour, you were made a child of God, or a child of light, but you must choose daily to live in such a way that God's light is revealed (John 12:35-36). Paul, while encouraging the believers in Ephesus to reject the darkness of sin in their lives, said, "***For ye were sometimes darkness, but now are ye light in the Lord: walk as children of light....Proving what is acceptable unto the Lord....Wherefore he saith, Awake thou that sleepest, and arise from the dead, and Christ shall give thee light. See then that ye***

The Christian's Walk

walk circumspectly, not as fools, but as wise, redeeming the time, because the days are evil" (Ephesians 5:8-17). While Christ was on the earth, He was "*the light of the world*" (John 9:5). However, now that He has ascended into heaven, Matthew 5:14-16 says, "*Ye are the light of the world. A city that is set on an hill cannot be hid. Neither do men light a candle, and put it under a bushel, but on a candlestick; and it giveth light unto all that are in the house. Let your light so shine before men, that they may see your good works, and glorify your Father which is in heaven.*" Christ has given you His light of righteous living so that you might be able to represent God, as your Father, to the dark world around you through your righteous activities. Therefore, walking in the light includes representing God and His truth, and it requires walking circumspectly.

Walking in the Light through Fellowship with Others

In Ephesians 5:8, Paul commanded the believers to "*walk as children of light.*" Previously in verses one and two he commanded them to "*Be ye therefore followers of God, as dear children; And walk in love, as Christ also hath loved us, and hath given himself for us an offering and a sacrifice to God for a sweetsmelling savour.*" Christ displayed His love for you by selflessly sacrificing Himself to pay for your sins. Therefore, after receiving His gift of love, becoming a child of light, and then reflecting His righteousness, you should be willing to love those around you.

Paul then revealed in part how your walking in love will guide you to walk in light, saying, "*But fornication, and all uncleanness, or covetousness, let it not be once named among you, as becometh saints; Neither filthiness, nor foolish talking, nor jesting, which are not convenient: but rather giving of thanks*" (Ephesians 5:3-4). Loving others as Christ has loved you will prevent you from sinning with or against them. Romans 13:10 explains, "*Love worketh no ill to his neighbour: therefore love is the fulfilling of the law.*" Romans 14:13-15 adds, "*Let us not

Walking in the Light

therefore judge one another any more: but judge this rather, that no man put a stumblingblock or an occasion to fall in his brother's way....But if thy brother be grieved with thy meat, now walkest thou not charitably. Destroy not him with thy meat, for whom Christ died." In the early church there were conflicts over what meat could be eaten because of the Jewish traditions. Some believers thought that they could only eat meat approved of by the law of Moses, whereas others understood that such rules no longer applied. Paul resolves the problem by teaching that neither party should judge the other, but rather that each should seek to not offend the other and thereby demonstrate Christ-like love.

As mentioned in the introduction, John revealed in I John 2:9-11 that not loving your brother is equal to walking in darkness, saying, "*He that saith he is in the light, and hateth his brother, is in darkness even until now. He that loveth his brother abideth in the light, and there is none occasion of stumbling in him. But he that hateth his brother is in darkness, and walketh in darkness, and knoweth not whither he goeth, because that darkness hath blinded his eyes.*" In II John 1:4-6, John explained the connection between walking in the light and walking in love saying, "*I rejoiced greatly that I found of thy children walking in truth, as we have received a commandment from the Father. And now I beseech thee, lady, not as though I wrote a new commandment unto thee, but that which we had from the beginning, that we love one another. And this is love, that we walk after his commandments. This is the commandment, That, as ye have heard from the beginning, ye should walk in it.*" John was connecting the dots. Walking in the light is walking in Christ's righteousness based on God the Father's truth. Because God commanded you to walk in love with those around you, you are walking in the light when you obey God's commandment and love as God has loved you. But John did not end by commanding the believers to walk in love so they might walk in light. In III John 1:4-6, he praised their actions of love that they had accomplished as they walked in the truth of God's commandment

54

The Christian's Walk

to love. He wrote, "*I have no greater joy than to hear that my children walk in truth. Beloved, thou doest faithfully whatsoever thou doest to the brethren, and to strangers; Which have borne witness of thy charity before the church: whom if thou bring forward on their journey after a godly sort, thou shalt do well*" (III John 1:4-6). As you dedicate yourself to walk in the light by loving others, you can be assured that "*God is not unrighteous to forget your work and labour of love, which ye have shewed toward his name, in that ye have ministered to the saints, and do minister*" (Hebrews 6:10).

Walking in the Light Is a Personal Choice

The New Testament's teaching on walking in light reveals the wonderful truth that you are a child of light because you are a child of God through your faith in Jesus Christ. However, it also commands you to continually live within God's light by living righteously and maintaining proper relationships with God the Father and others. Are you living in agreement with God's truths by obeying His commands? Are you being circumspect in your words, actions, and attitude? Are you maintaining a proper relationship with others by loving them the way Christ loved you? What areas of your life have become dark with sin because you have not allowed God's light to guide your attitudes, actions, or words? What changes in your life must you make so that you can reflect God's light in your day-to-day activities?

The Christian's Walk

Biblical Principles about Walking in the Light

- ✓ **John 11:9-10** - Those who walk in darkness will stumble and fall.

- ✓ **Thessalonians 5:4-8** - Christians are children of light and are not to live as children of darkness.

- ✓ **I Peter 2:9-11** - Christians have been called out of sin's darkness into God's light and are to live as pilgrims on this earth.

- ✓ **James 4:3** - Friendship with the world is contrary to friendship with God.

- ✓ **Philippians 2:15-16** - Christians are to live as lights by following God's Word in the midst of the world's wickedness.

- ✓ **John 17:13-18** - Christians are not of the world and must be sanctified by God's Word, the Word of Truth.

- ✓ **I John 2:15-17** - Christians are not to love the world because it is temporal; instead, they are to love God Who is eternal.

- ✓ **Romans 13:9-10** - All of God's commandments for interpersonal relationships are summed up in loving others as yourself.

- ✓ **I John 3:14-18** - Christians are to love others as God has loved them and gave Himself for them.

Walking in the Light

- ✓ _____ - _____
- ✓ _____ - _____
- ✓ _____ - _____
- ✓ _____ - _____
- ✓ _____ - _____
- ✓ _____ - _____
- ✓ _____ - _____
- ✓ _____ - _____
- ✓ _____ - _____
- ✓ _____ - _____
- ✓ _____ - _____
- ✓ _____ - _____

Biblical Investigation about Walking in the Light

✎ Bible Reading: John 8:12, 12:35-47, Romans 13:12-14, 14:13-15, II Corinthians 4:1-2, Ephesians 5:1-14, I John 1:5-9, 2:7-11, II John 1:4-6, III John 1:3-6
✎ Bible Memory Verses: Ephesians 5:8
8 For ye were sometimes darkness, but now are ye light in the Lord: walk as children of light:

1. Walking in the light is a lifestyle of living in a <u>agreement</u> with Jesus Christ's <u>righteousness</u> by maintaining a proper relationship with God the <u>Father</u> by walking in His <u>truth</u> and having a proper relationship with <u>others</u> by walking in <u>love</u>.

2. Who is the light of the world? (John 8:12; see also John 1:1-13, 9:5, 12:46)
   <u>Jesus Christ</u>
   What do you have to do in order to have His light of life?
   <u>Follow Him - Believe in Him</u>

3. What did you become when you believed in Jesus Christ? (John 12:35-36)
   <u>A child of light</u>

4. What are the two Great Commandments? (Matthew 22:37-40)
   a <u>Love God with all your heart, soul, and mind</u>
   b <u>Love thy neighbor as yourself</u>
   What do the two Great Commandments fulfill?
   <u>All the law and prophets</u>

Walking in the Light

5. What does walking in truth require? (II John 1:4-6)
   Obeying God's commandments
   What specific commandment did God give you in this passage?
   Love my brother

6. What are you walking in if you do not love your brother? (I John 2:9-11)
   Darkness
   What danger comes from not loving your brother?
   I won't know where I'm going

Walking in the Light through Fellowship with God the Father

7. Why do many men not walk in light? (John 3:16-21)
   Because their deeds are evil, and they reject the truth
   ☞ What are some evil deeds that men try to cover up with darkness or lies?

   ☞ What are some areas of your life that you do not want to be revealed by God's light of truth?

8. Does God the Father have any darkness in Him? (I John 1:5-9)
   Yes / No
   Can you walk in darkness and have fellowship with God the Father?
   Yes / No
   What must you allow to cleanse you from your sins so that you can have fellowship with God the Father?
   Jesus Christ's blood

The Christian's Walk

☞ Are you willing to confess the areas of your life in which God says you have been walking in darkness and allow Jesus Christ to cleanse your sins?
Yes / No

9. What are you to do with the works of darkness? (Romans 13:12-14)
   Cast them off
   What are some of the works of darkness listed in this passage?
   a   Rioting
   b   Drunkenness
   c   Chambering
   d   Wantonness
   e   Strife
   f   Envying
   What are you to put on?
   The armour of light
   What must be displayed in your daily living if your are going to walk in light?
   Honestly
   ☞ Are there any areas of your life in which you have not been honest? What must you do to resolve your dishonesty?

10. What are you to do with the things of dishonesty if you are going to serve God? (II Corinthians 4:1-2)
    Renounce them
    What must you remove from your daily living if you are going to serve God?
    Craftiness
    What must you manifest if your are going to serve God and others?
    The truth

Study Guide - Page 97

Walking in the Light

11. Does righteousness and unrighteousness have fellowship? (II Corinthians 6:14-18)
    Yes / No
    Do light and darkness have fellowship?
    Yes / No
    What does God the Father promise you if you separate yourself from unrighteousness/darkness?
    He will receive me as one of His children
    ☞ What human relationships or practices are preventing you from enjoying your relationship with God, your heavenly Father?

    _____
    _____

12. How did you live before you received Jesus Christ's light? (Ephesians 5:8-16)
    In darkness
    When you live in the light, you are acceptable to Whom?
    Jesus Christ
    How are you to walk so that you stay living in the light?
    Circumspectly - wisely
    ☞ What areas of your old life of walking in darkness must you confess and change so that your new life is acceptable to Jesus Christ?

    _____
    _____

13. Who has replaced Jesus Christ as the light of the world after His ascension into heaven? (Matthew 5:14-16)
    I have - believers
    What must I do in order for your light to shine before others?
    Good works

The Christian's Walk

Who must you receive the glory from your light shining?
God the Father

☞ What are some good works that you can do that will reveal your light and glorify God the Father before others?

_____
_____

Walking in the Light through Fellowship with Others

14. As a child of God, Who should you follow? (Ephesians 5:1-8)
    God the Father
    Who is your example of walking in love?
    Jesus Christ
    What types of things will not be part of your life when you walk in love?
    a   Fornication
    b   Uncleanness
    c   Covetousness
    d   Filthiness
    e   Foolish talking
    f   Jesting
    What will be part of your life when you walk in love?
    Giving thanks
    ☞ What are some ways in which you can display your love for others?

    _____
    _____

15. What one thing will love never do? (Romans 13:10)
    Ill - Sin

Walking in the Light

16. What should you not put in a fellows believer's way if you truly love them? (Romans 14:13-15)
    <u>A stumbling block</u>
    ☞ What are some beliefs or practices that some believer's might understand differently?

    ☞ How can you show Christ-like love to fellow believers when there are differences of views about everyday practices like eating?

17. What is the difference between those who love and those who do not? (I John 2:9-11)
    9 He that saith he is in the <u>light</u>, and <u>hateth</u> his brother, is in <u>darkness</u> even until now.
    10 He that <u>loveth</u> his brother abideth in the <u>light</u>, and there is none occasion of <u>stumbling</u> in him.
    11 But he that <u>hateth</u> his brother is in <u>darkness</u>, and walketh in <u>darkness</u>, and <u>knoweth</u> not whither he goeth, because that darkness hath <u>blinded</u> his eyes.
    ☞ In what ways do you stumble into the darkness of sin because you do not love others correctly?

18. What does walking in truth require? (II John 1:4-6, III John 1:4-6)
    <u>Obeying God's commandment</u>
    What is God's commandment that you must obey?
    <u>Love one another</u>

The Christian's Walk

19. Who will reward you for your works of love to others? (Hebrews 6:10)
    God

Walking in the Light
Is a Personal Choice

20. Are there areas of your life that should be changed so you can be walking in the light? What are those areas, and what changes should you make? Will you ask God for His help to make these changes?

Personal Notes about Waking in Light

Walking in the Light

Chapter 6

Walking in the Spirit

Romans 8:1-17
1 There is therefore now no condemnation
to them which are in Christ Jesus,
who walk not after the flesh, but after the Spirit.
4 That the righteousness of the law might be fulfilled in
us, who walk not after the flesh, but after the Spirit.

I Corinthians 3:1-4
3 For ye are yet carnal:
for whereas there is among you envying,
and strife, and divisions,
are ye not carnal, and walk as men?

II Corinthians 10:1-7
2 ...as if we walked according to the flesh.
3 For though we walk in the flesh,
we do not war after the flesh:
4 (For the weapons of our warfare are not carnal,
but mighty through God
to the pulling down of strong holds;)

Galatians 5:13-26
16 This I say then, Walk in the Spirit,
and ye shall not fulfil the lust of the flesh.
24 And they that are Christ's
have crucified the flesh with the affections and lusts.
25 If we live in the Spirit,
let us also walk in the Spirit.

Chapter 6

Walking in the Spirit

Romans 8:1-17
I Corinthians 3:1-4
II Corinthians 10:1-7
Galatians 5:13-26

Biblical Instruction about Walking in the Spirit

In Romans 8:14-17, the apostle Paul revealed that God's children have all been given the privilege of being indwelt by God's Spirit, saying, *"For as many as are led by the Spirit of God, they are the sons of God. For ye have not received the spirit of bondage again to fear; but ye have received the Spirit of adoption, whereby we cry, Abba, Father. The Spirit itself beareth witness with our spirit, that we are the children of God: And if children, then heirs; heirs of God, and joint-heirs with Christ; if so be that we suffer with him, that we may be also glorified together."* At the moment of your salvation, you received the Holy Spirit for the purpose of reassuring you that God is your "Abba," or Daddy, to guide and empower you to live as an obedient child (John 14, 15, 16, Acts 1:8).

In Romans 8:1-4, Paul boldly declared, *"There is therefore now no condemnation to them which are in Christ Jesus, who walk not after the flesh, but after the Spirit. For the law of the Spirit of life in Christ Jesus hath made me free from the law of sin and death. For what the law could not do, in that it was weak through the flesh, God sending his own Son in the likeness of sinful flesh, and for sin, condemned sin in the flesh: That the*

Walking in the Spirit

righteousness of the law might be fulfilled in us, who walk not after the flesh, but after the Spirit." As discovered in chapter six, "Walking in Newness of Life," you have been freed from the authority and penalty of sin so that you might live in obedience to righteousness. In Romans 8:5-8, Paul explained, saying, "*For they that are after the flesh do mind the things of the flesh; but they that are after the Spirit the things of the Spirit. For to be carnally minded is death; but to be spiritually minded is life and peace. Because the carnal mind is enmity against God: for it is not subject to the law of God, neither indeed can be. So then they that are in the flesh cannot please God.*" Living according to the desires of the flesh, or in carnality of the mind, will always result in a life of death and despair because it is not pleasing to God the Father. But living according to the guidance of the Holy Spirit will always result in a blessed life and personal peace because it is pleasing to God the Father.

Paul assured the believers in Rome that they did not need to fear the destruction that a fleshly life produces by reminding them of their new life in Jesus Christ, saying, "*But ye are not in the flesh, but in the Spirit, if so be that the Spirit of God dwell in you. Now if any man have not the Spirit of Christ, he is none of his. And if Christ be in you, the body is dead because of sin; but the Spirit is life because of righteousness. But if the Spirit of him that raised up Jesus from the dead dwell in you, he that raised up Christ from the dead shall also quicken your mortal bodies by his Spirit that dwelleth in you. Therefore, brethren, we are debtors, not to the flesh, to live after the flesh. For if ye live after the flesh, ye shall die: but if ye through the Spirit do mortify the deeds of the body, ye shall live*" (Romans 8:9-13). Although you still live in a body made of flesh and blood, Paul revealed that your body has been quickened, or made alive, by the indwelling of the Holy Spirit. This means that although your body was committed to sin before your salvation, at the moment you became a child of God, your body was given resurrection power to reject the desires of your flesh and accept the direction of the Holy

The Christian's Walk

Spirit. You now have the ability to choose how you're going to live: according to the flesh or according to the Spirit.

In II Corinthians 10:2-6, Paul, while speaking of his own life and ministry said, "*I think to be bold against some, which think of us as if we walked according to the flesh. For though we walk in the flesh, we do not war after the flesh: (For the weapons of our warfare are not carnal, but mighty through God to the pulling down of strong holds;). Casting down imaginations, and every high thing that exalteth itself against the knowledge of God, and bringing into captivity every thought to the obedience of Christ; And having in a readiness to revenge all disobedience, when your obedience is fulfilled.*" He was clear that although he was still living in his earthly body, he was not depending on his carnal flesh to fight his spiritual battles. He was depending on God's strength to remove those things in His life and ministry that would distract him and those around him from growing in their knowledge of God the Father and in obeying Christ. Sadly, some of the believers in Corinth were not committed to living the same way, and Paul had to strongly rebuke them, saying, "*And I, brethren, could not speak unto you as unto spiritual, but as unto carnal, even as unto babes in Christ. I have fed you with milk, and not with meat: for hitherto ye were not able to bear it, neither yet now are ye able. For ye are yet carnal: for whereas there is among you envying, and strife, and divisions, are ye not carnal, and walk as men? For while one saith, I am of Paul; and another, I am of Apollos; are ye not carnal?*" (I Corinthians 3:1-4). If you choose to live according to your flesh, you will not grow spiritually, and you will find your life filled with constant conflict. You have been saved from that type of living. God has forgiven your past sins and has given you an opportunity to choose to separate yourself from your old habits. *Walking in the Spirit is a lifestyle that rejects the flesh's sinful desires by allowing the Holy Spirit to guide one's attitudes and actions to do that which pleases God in each daily activity.*

Walking in the Spirit Rejects the Works of the Flesh

In Galatians 5:16-17, Paul made a universal statement, saying, *"Walk in the Spirit, and ye shall not fulfil the lust of the flesh. For the flesh lusteth against the Spirit, and the Spirit against the flesh: and these are contrary the one to the other: so that ye cannot do the things that ye would."* Without question, to walk in the Spirit is the exact opposite of walking in the flesh. The two cannot be accomplished at the same time because they are enemies. Therefore, you cannot be following the Holy Spirit's guidance and relying on His power while doing something that is carnal, or sinful.

Paul continued by providing some common examples of the works of the flesh. In Galatians 5:19-21 he wrote, *"Now the works of the flesh are manifest, which are these; Adultery, fornication, uncleanness, lasciviousness, idolatry, witchcraft, hatred, variance, emulations, wrath, strife, seditions, heresies, envyings, murders, drunkenness, revellings, and such like: of the which I tell you before, as I have also told you in time past, that they which do such things shall not inherit the kingdom of God."* Paul's lists of sins are the reason mankind needed Christ's salvation and are the very sins that God saved you from (Ephesians 2:1-5). This list of sins includes sexual sins, religious sins, attitudinal sins, verbal sins, social sins, *"and such like"* (Galatians 5:21). Although this list of sins is very extensive, it does not include every sin that the flesh may tempt you to commit. However, it does reflect the sins that many believers attempt to not commit in their own strength and fail.

In II Peter 2:10-18, the apostle Peter, while warning the believers of the influence of false teachers, described those who walk in the flesh as *"them that walk after the flesh in the lust of uncleanness, and despise government. Presumptuous are they, selfwilled, they are not afraid to speak evil of dignities [and to] speak evil of the things that they understand not…as they that count it pleasure to riot in the day time. Spots they are and blemishes, sporting themselves with their own deceivings while they feast with you; Having eyes full of adultery, and that cannot cease from sin; beguiling unstable souls: an heart they have exercised with covetous practices; cursed children: Which have forsaken the right way, and are gone astray...they speak great swelling words of vanity, they allure through the lusts of the flesh, through much wantonness.*" Although the above description is quite grotesque and always leads to God's judgment, Peter reassures you by saying, "*The Lord knoweth how to deliver the godly out of temptations*" (II Peter 2:9).

By placing your faith in Christ as your personal Savior, you have been freed from the power of your flesh and are not required to live according to its desires. Peter wrote, "*Dearly beloved, I beseech you as strangers and pilgrims, abstain from fleshly lusts, which war against the soul*" (I Peter 2:11). Paul added, "*Having therefore these promises, dearly beloved, let us cleanse ourselves from all filthiness of the flesh and spirit, perfecting holiness in the fear of God*" (II Corinthians 7:1). You do not need to follow your flesh's desires, which will lead you to commit sins that you will later regret. Rather, the Bible says to "*put ye on the Lord Jesus Christ, and make not provision for the flesh, to fulfil the lusts thereof*" (Romans 13:14). Galatians 5:24 declares that "*they that are Christ's have crucified the flesh with the affections and lusts.*" By remembering and relying on Christ's saving power, you can reject temptation and follow the guidance of the Holy Spirit to produce fruits of righteousness.

Walking in the Spirit Accepts the Guidance of the Holy Spirit
In Galatians 5:25, Paul was writing to believers who had been indwelt by the Holy Spirit at their salvation (just as you have been) and said, "*If we live in the Spirit, let us also walk in the Spirit.*" Every believer lives in or under the influence of the Holy Spirit, but they must also choose to walk in fellowship with the Spirit, allowing Him to guide their day-to-day attitudes and actions. When the Holy Spirit has such an influence over a believer's life, He produces spiritual fruit that cannot be produced

Walking in the Spirit

by any other source. In Galatians 5:22-23, Paul listed the Spirit's fruit as being *"**love, joy, peace, longsuffering, gentleness, goodness, faith, meekness, [and] temperance.**"* Paul then stated, *"**against such there is no law**"* because it *"**is in all goodness and righteousness and truth**"* (Galatians 5:22-23, Ephesians 5:9). Although there are plenty of human laws intended to prevent the works of the flesh listed previously, there is no human law that can prevent the Holy Spirit from producing His fruit in your life. As well, there is no human source that can fully provide you with such fruit. You must choose to allow the Holy Spirit to produce these characteristics in you.

Physical fruit such as apples or grapes must be cultivated. They do not develop based on their own will nor due to their own strength; they must be sown as a seed and then depend on a tree or a vine for growth. The same is true for the fruit of the Spirit. Galatians 6:7-8 says, *"**Be not deceived; God is not mocked: for whatsoever a man soweth, that shall he also reap. For he that soweth to his flesh shall of the flesh reap corruption; but he that soweth to the Spirit shall of the Spirit reap life everlasting.**"* Sowing to the flesh involves focusing one's life on those things that the flesh desires, whereas sowing to the Spirit is focusing one's life on being around those things that the Spirit desires. In John 14:16-17, Jesus says *"**I will pray the Father, and he shall give you another Comforter, that he may abide with you for ever; Even the Spirit of truth; whom the world cannot receive, because it seeth him not, neither knoweth him: but ye know him; for he dwelleth with you, and shall be in you.**"* He also said in John 15:26-27, *"**But when the Comforter is come, whom I will send unto you from the Father, even the Spirit of truth, which proceedeth from the Father, he shall testify of me: And ye also shall bear witness, because ye have been with me from the beginning.**"* Finally, in John 16:13-14 He said, *"**Howbeit when he, the Spirit of truth, is come, he will guide you into all truth: for he shall not speak of himself; but whatsoever he shall hear, that shall he speak: and he will shew you things to come. He**

The Christian's Walk

shall glorify me: for he shall receive of mine, and shall shew it unto you." Therefore, according to Christ's promises, the Holy Spirit has the special ministry of comforting believers by teaching them God's truth and glorifying Christ (Acts 9:31).

As the Holy Spirit teaches you about Christ, He reveals the true sources of "*love, joy, peace, longsuffering, gentleness, goodness, faith, meekness, [and] temperance*" (Galatians 5:22-23). First, Jesus taught true love, saying, "*Greater love hath no man than this, that a man lay down his life for his friends,*" which He then personally demonstrated when He "*gave himself for us, that he might redeem us from all iniquity*" (John 15:13, I Timothy 2:6). Second, Jesus taught His disciples about true joy when He said, "*These things have I spoken unto you, that my joy might remain in you, and that your joy might be full*" (John 15:11). Third, after promising the Holy Spirit as a Comforter, Jesus said, "*Peace I leave with you, my peace I give unto you: not as the world giveth, give I unto you. Let not your heart be troubled, neither let it be afraid*" (John 14:27). Fourth, Jesus demonstrated true longsuffering as "*the longsuffering of our Lord is salvation*" (II Peter 3:15). Fifth, God the Father displayed "*his grace in his kindness [or gentleness] toward us through Christ Jesus*" (Ephesians 2:7). Sixth, Jesus was called "*Good Master*" and "*did no sin, neither was guile found in his mouth*" (Mark 10:17, I Peter 2:22), thus demonstrating goodness. Seventh, Jesus is the source of our faith, being called "*the author and finisher of our faith*" (Hebrews 12:2). Eighth, Jesus described himself as meek when he said, "*Come unto me, all ye that labour and are heavy laden, and I will give you rest. Take my yoke upon you, and learn of me; for I am meek and lowly in heart: and ye shall find rest unto your souls. For my yoke is easy, and my burden is light*" (Matthew 11:28-30). Finally, Jesus displayed complete temperance as He could have called "*more than twelve legions of angels*" to rescue Him from the cross but instead chose to be crucified to save you from your sins (Matthew 26:53). Therefore, as you walk in the Spirit, He will guide you to grow in your

Walking in the Spirit

knowledge of God's truth about Christ so that His characteristics begin to develop in your daily life.

Walking in the Spirit Is a Personal Choice

The New Testament's teaching on walking in the Spirit reveals that you are indwelt by the Holy Spirit at the moment of your faith in Christ as your personal Savior. It also teaches that walking in the Spirit is a life-long process by which you reject the works of the flesh and allow the Holy Spirit to develop Jesus's characteristics in your life. Have you trusted in Christ as your personal Savior so that you can enjoy the Holy Spirit's continual comfort? Are you consistently rejecting the fleshly desire to live for your own interests rather than according to God's Word? Are you allowing the Holy Spirit to develop Jesus Christ's nine characteristics in you as you confront life's diverse circumstances? What changes do you need to make so that you can enjoy the Holy Spirit's fruit?

The Christian's Walk

Biblical Instruction about Walking in the Spirit

✓ **I Corinthians 2:9-14** - The Holy Spirit teaches Christians things that the world cannot understand.

✓ **Romans 6:20-22** - The fruit of fleshly sinful works produce shame, but the fruit of righteousness is holiness.

✓ **Romans 7:1-25** - Jesus Christ is the only solution for man's battle against his fleshly desires.

✓ **Ephesians 4:17-32** - Christians are to walk differently than the world by putting off the old man and putting on the new man, which they learn from Jesus.

✓ **Colossians 3:5-10** - Christians are to walk differently than before they were saved by putting to death their fleshly, sinful desires as they put on the new man, which is made in the image of Jesus Christ.

✓ **I Peter 4:1-3** - Christians are to walk differently than when they were unsaved and followed the desires of the flesh.

✓ **Ephesians 5:18-21** - Christians are to be filled with the Holy Spirit, allowing Him to control their attitudes and actions.

✓ _____ - _____

✓ _____ - _____

Walking in the Spirit

- ✓ _____ - _____
- ✓ _____ - _____
- ✓ _____ - _____
- ✓ _____ - _____
- ✓ _____ - _____
- ✓ _____ - _____
- ✓ _____ - _____
- ✓ _____ - _____
- ✓ _____ - _____
- ✓ _____ - _____
- ✓ _____ - _____
- ✓ _____ - _____

The Christian's Walk

Biblical Investigation about Walking in the Spirit

✎ Bible Reading: Romans 8:1-17, I Corinthians 3:1-4,
   II Corinthians 10:1-17, Galatians 5:13-26
✎ Bible Memory Verses: Galatians 5:16
   16 This I say then, Walk in the Spirit, and ye shall not fulfil the lust of the flesh.

1. Walking in the Spirit is a lifestyle that <u>rejects</u> the <u>flesh's</u> sinful desires by allowing the <u>Holy</u> <u>Spirit</u> to guide one's <u>attitudes</u> and <u>actions</u> to do that which <u>pleases</u> <u>God</u> in each daily activity.

2. What has been eliminated from your life if you walk in the Spirit? (Romans 8:1-17, Galatians 4:5-6)
   Condemnation
   From what has the Holy Spirit made you free?
   The law of sin
   When you walk in the Spirit, you will not be walking in what?
   The flesh
   Of what does the Holy Spirit assure you?
   That I am a child of God
   What can you call God the Father because His Spirit is in you?
   Abba Father

3. Whose strength will help you win your spiritual battles when you walk in the Spirit? (II Corinthians 10:2-6)
   God's
   What will you do with your thoughts if you walk in the Spirit?
   Bring them into captivity for the purpose of obeying Jesus Christ

Walking in the Spirit

☞ What subjects in your thought life need to be brought under better control?
_____
_____

4. What do envying, strife, and divisions reveal about your spiritual walk? (I Corinthians 3:1-4)
   <u>It is carnal</u>
   ☞ Are there specific relationships in which you often display your carnality?
   _____
   _____

   ☞ What are some steps that you can take to correct your carnality in the above relationships?
   _____
   _____

Walking in the Spirit
Rejects the Works of the Flesh

5. Can you walk in the Spirit and the flesh at the same time? (Galatians 5:16-21)
   Yes / No
   What are the works of the flesh that are named in this passage?

a	Adultery	j	Wrath
b	Fornication	k	Strife
c	Uncleanness	l	Seditions
d	Lasciviousness	m	Heresies
e	Idolatry	n	Envyings
f	Witchcraft	o	Murders
g	Hatred	p	Drunkenness
h	Variance	q	Revellings
i	Emulations	r	Such like

The Christian's Walk

☞ What are some other works of the flesh that might be described by the phrase "and such the like?"
_____
_____

☞ What are some of the areas in which you struggle with temptations in your flesh?
_____
_____

6. Who saved you from living according to your flesh? (Ephesians 2:1-5)
   <u>Jesus Christ</u>

7. How does Peter describe those who walk in the flesh? (II Peter 2:10-18)
   10 But chiefly them that walk after the flesh in the lust of <u>uncleanness</u>, and <u>despise</u> government. <u>Presumptuous</u> are they, <u>selfwilled</u>, they are not afraid to speak <u>evil</u> of <u>dignities</u>.
   12 ...speak <u>evil</u> of the things that they <u>understand</u> not...
   13 ...as they that count it <u>pleasure</u> to <u>riot</u> in the day time. Spots they are and blemishes, <u>sporting</u> themselves with their own <u>deceivings</u> while they feast with you;
   14 Having eyes full of <u>adultery</u>, and that cannot <u>cease from sin</u>; <u>beguiling</u> unstable souls: an <u>heart</u> they have <u>exercised</u> with <u>covetous</u> practices; cursed children:
   15 Which have <u>forsaken</u> the <u>right</u> way, and are gone <u>astray</u>...
   18 ...they speak great swelling <u>words</u> of vanity, they <u>allure</u> through the lusts of the <u>flesh</u>, through much <u>wantonness</u>...
   ☞ Does walking according to the flesh sound very appealing?
   Yes / No

8. Who knows how to save you from walking in the flesh? (II Peter 2:9)
   <u>The Lord</u>

Walking in the Spirit

9. Against what do fleshly lusts war? (I Peter 2:11)
   My own soul
   What are you to do with fleshly lusts?
   Abstain from them
   ☞ What are some ways that you can abstain from your own fleshly desires?

   _____

   _____

10. Because you have been given God's promises to be with you as a father, what should you do with the filthiness of the flesh? (II Corinthians 7:1)
    Cleanse myself from it

11. For what must you not make provision? (Romans 13:14)
    For the flesh–to fulfill its lusts
    ☞ What are some ways that you can prevent the flesh from having an opportunity to tempt you?

    _____

    _____

12. What was crucified with Christ when you accepted Him as your personal Savior? (Galatians 5:24)
    The flesh with its affections and lusts

Walking in the Spirit
Accepts the Guidance of the Holy Spirit

13. How should you walk if your are living in or with the Holy Spirit? (Galatians 5:22-25, Acts 9:31)
    In the Spirit

The Christian's Walk

What is the fruit of the Spirit?
a Love
b Joy
c Peace
d Longsuffering
e Gentleness
f Goodness
g Faith
h Meekness
i Temperance

Are there any laws that limits the fruit of the Spirit?
Yes / No

☞ Do you regularly display the above characteristics?
Yes / No

☞ What are some areas of your life in which you need to display the fruit of the Spirit more?

_____
_____

14. What is the fruit of the Spirit based on? (Ephesians 5:9)
    a Goodness
    b Righteousness
    c Truth

15. What will you receive if you sow to the flesh? (Galatians 6:7-8)
    Corruption
    What will you receive if you sow to the Spirit?
    Life everlasting

16. What are the two other names that Jesus used for the Holy Spirit? (John 14:16-17)
    a Comforter
    b Spirit of truth

Walking in the Spirit

How long will the Holy Spirit be with you?
Forever
Where does the Holy Spirit dwell?
In me
Are you enjoying the comfort of the Holy Spirit on a daily basis?
Yes / No
Are you learning God's truth from the Holy Spirit on a daily basis?
Yes / No

17. Of whom will the Holy Spirit testify? (John 15:26-27)
    Jesus Christ

18. What will the Holy Spirit guide you to know? (John 16:13-14)
    Truth
    Of whom will the Holy Spirit speak?
    Jesus Christ
    Whom will the Holy Spirit glorify?
    Jesus Christ

19. Match the passages of Scripture that reveal Jesus Christ's teaching or example for the nine parts of the fruit of the Spirit.

a	_6_	Love	1	Matthew 11:28-30
b	_5_	Joy	2	Matthew 26:53
c	_4_	Peace	3	Mark 10:17-18, I Peter 2:22
d	_8_	Longsuffering	4	John 14:27
e	_7_	Gentleness	5	John 15:11
f	_3_	Goodness	6	John 15:13, I Timothy 2:6
g	_9_	Faith	7	Ephesians 2:7
h	_1_	Meekness	8	II Peter 3:15
i	_2_	Temperance	9	Hebrews 12:2

The Christian's Walk

Whose example are you to follow throughout your Christian life?
Jesus Christ

What are some areas of your life that need to change in order to follow Jesus Christ's example?

_____

_____

**Walking in the Spirit
Is a Personal Choice**

20. Are there areas of your life that should be changed so you can be walking in the Spirit? What are those areas, and what changes should you make? Will you ask God for His help to make these changes?

_____

_____

_____

_____

_____

_____

_____

_____

_____

_____

_____

_____

_____

_____

_____

Personal Notes about Walking in the Spirit

Chapter 7

Walking Where You Are Called
Walking in the Fear of the Lord
Walking According to the Gospel

Acts 9:31
Then had the churches rest
throughout all Judaea and Galilee and Samaria,
and were edified;
and walking in the fear of the Lord,
and in the comfort of the Holy Ghost,
were multiplied.

I Corinthians 7:10-24
17 But as God hath distributed to every man,
as the Lord hath called every one,
so let him walk. And so ordain I in all churches.
20 Let every man abide in the same calling
wherein he was called.
24 Brethren, let every man,
wherein he is called,
therein abide with God.

Galatians 2:14-16
14 But when I saw that they walked not uprightly
according to the truth of the gospel,
I said unto Peter before them all,
If thou, being a Jew,
livest after the manner of Gentiles,
and not as do the Jews,
why compellest thou the Gentiles
to live as do the Jews?

Chapter 7

Walking Where You Are Called
Walking in the Fear of the Lord
Walking According to the Gospel

Acts 9:31
I Corinthians 7:12-24
Galatians 2:14-16

A Biblical Instruction about Walking Where You Are Called

In I Corinthians 7:17, the apostle Paul commanded the believers in Corinth, saying, "*But as God hath distributed to every man, as the Lord hath called every one, so let him walk. And so ordain I in all churches.*" Earlier in his letter, he had informed them that they were "*called to be saints,*" being "*called unto the fellowship,*" "*both Jews and Greeks*" as "*brethren*" regardless of their social status (I Corinthians 1:2, 9, 24, 26). Their calling had come from their acceptance of Christ as their Savior, which made them all part of God's family and His kingdom of light and holiness (John 1:12, I John 3:1-3, I Peter 2:9-10). However, that did not mean that their earthly circumstances would immediately change. In I Corinthians 7:10-24, Paul gives three general circumstances in which believers must choose to live out their new calling as saints: in their families, in their cultures, and in their employment.

In each of life's circumstances, God commands believers to "*therein abide with God*" as they "*abide in the same calling wherein [they are] called*" (I Corinthians 7:20, 24). Although your

Walking where You Are Called

lifestyle should clearly be different than before your salvation, you are to allow those changes to take place while maintaining your established relationships and responsibilities as long as they do not violate God's Word (I Corinthians 5:9-11, Philippians 2:15-16). By doing so, you will become a testimony of God's love and salvation to those who still need to accept Him for themselves. Although the early church suffered great persecution, after God gave them deliverance, the Bible records that the believers displayed a godly testimony in their communities by *"walking in the fear of the Lord, and in the comfort of the Holy Ghost" and the number of believers was "multiplied"* (Acts 9:31). Jesus said it this way in His High-Priestly prayer: *"I pray not that thou shouldest take them out of the world, but that thou shouldest keep them from the evil"* (John 17:15). *Walking where you are called is a lifestyle of godliness within your already-established relationships and responsibilities.*

Walking Where You Are Called in Your Family

In I Corinthians 7:12-17, Paul addressed walking where you are called within the family context. In verses ten and eleven, Paul taught that saved couples should work together to stay together, saying, *"And unto the married I command, yet not I, but the Lord, Let not the wife depart from her husband: But and if she depart, let her remain unmarried, or be reconciled to her husband: and let not the husband put away his wife."* He then continued by addressing the complex yet realistic circumstance of one spouse becoming a believer with the other remaining an unbeliever. In this case, Paul said, *"If any brother hath a wife that believeth not, and she be pleased to dwell with him, let him not put her away. And the woman which hath an husband that believeth not, and if he be pleased to dwell with her, let her not leave him...But if the unbelieving depart, let him depart. A brother or a sister is not under bondage in such cases: but God hath called us to peace"* (I Corinthian 7:12-13). Therefore, a saved spouse must always seek to remain in the place of their

74

The Christian's Walk

calling, being married, unless the unbelieving spouse chooses otherwise. If the unbelieving spouse chooses to leave, the saved spouse is to allow them to go peaceably.

Paul provided two reasons for staying within a marriage, even when one spouse remains unsaved. I Corinthians 7:14-16 says, "*For the unbelieving husband is sanctified by the wife, and the unbelieving wife is sanctified by the husband...For what knowest thou, O wife, whether thou shalt save thy husband? or how knowest thou, O man, whether thou shalt save thy wife?*" A believing spouse staying in the relationship with an unbelieving spouse provides a spiritual influence. The apostle Peter added further instruction saying, "*Likewise, ye wives, be in subjection to your own husbands; that, if any obey not the word, they also may without the word be won by the conversation of the wives; While they behold your chaste conversation coupled with fear. Whose adorning let it not be that outward adorning of plaiting the hair, and of wearing of gold, or of putting on of apparel; But let it be the hidden man of the heart, in that which is not corruptible, even the ornament of a meek and quiet spirit, which is in the sight of God of great price. Likewise, ye husbands, dwell with them according to knowledge, giving honour unto the wife, as unto the weaker vessel, and as being heirs together of the grace of life; that your prayers be not hindered*" (I Peter 3:1-7). When you choose to live as a child of God within a family that does not yet know God, you provide an opportunity for your family members to repent of their sins and turn to faith in and obedience to God. However, it is significant to note that Peter states that such an opportunity does not come by debating or demanding, but rather by a meek and loving godly lifestyle.

Paul also instructed believers to stay with their unbelieving spouses because of the spiritual influence they can have on their children. I Corinthians 7:14 says in part, "*Else were your children unclean; but now are they holy.*" God never desires for children to be raised in a broken home, which often produces resentment and rebellion. Therefore, although a believing spouse and an unbelieving spouse may approach parenting differently, the believing spouse is to peaceably maintain their marriage to keep their spiritual influence over their children so that they might become believers (Malachi 2:14-16).

In I Corinthians 7:17, Paul concluded by commanding, "*As God hath distributed to every man, as the Lord hath called every one, so let him walk.*" Therefore, you must consider your family relationships as opportunities to share the Gospel of Jesus Christ with those closest to you. You must not look to escape your circumstances but rather maintain a peaceful, God-honoring lifestyle that represents His holiness and love so that your family might be attracted to Christ and the change He can make in their lives.

Walking Where You Are Called in Your Culture

In I Corinthians 7:18-20, Paul continued his instruction about where a believer should live as a child of God, saying, "*Is any man called being circumcised? let him not become uncircumcised. Is any called in uncircumcision? let him not be circumcised. Circumcision is nothing, and uncircumcision is nothing, but the keeping of the commandments of God. Let every man abide in the same calling wherein he was called.*" Although circumcision was a religious act given by God to Abraham for the Jewish people, Christ removed the requirement of circumcision, making all those who believe in Him for their salvation new creatures regardless of their background (Romans 3:29-30, Galatians 5:6, 6:15, II Corinthians 5:17). Yet circumcision was such a distinguishing mark between the Jewish and Greek cultures that Paul had to defend the Gentile (Greek) culture (I Corinthians 1:22-24). In Galatians 2:14-16, Paul said, "*But when I saw that they walked not uprightly according to the truth of the gospel, I said unto Peter before them all, If thou, being a Jew, livest after the manner of Gentiles, and not as do the Jews, why compellest thou the Gentiles to live as do the Jews?…Knowing that a man is not justified by the works of the law, but by the faith of Jesus*

The Christian's Walk

Christ, even we have believed in Jesus Christ, that we might be justified by the faith of Christ, and not by the works of the law: for by the works of the law shall no flesh be justified." Therefore, Paul was instructing the early believers to no longer allow their cultural differences to be a point of separation regardless of the historical significance.

Paul's instruction about the removal of cultural distinctions was not an excuse for believers to practice those traditions that are clearly sinful, as he qualified his teaching by saying that they must still "*keep…the commandments of God*" (I Corinthians 7:19). In I Corinthians 9:20-23, Paul shared his own understanding and commitment to cultural distinctions when he said, "*For though I be free from all men, yet have I made myself servant unto all, that I might gain the more. And unto the Jews I became as a Jew, that I might gain the Jews; to them that are under the law, as under the law, that I might gain them that are under the law; To them that are without law, as without law, (being not without law to God, but under the law to Christ,) that I might gain them that are without law. To the weak became I as weak, that I might gain the weak: I am made all things to all men, that I might by all means save some. And this I do for the gospel's sake, that I might be partaker thereof with you.*" Paul was willing to sacrifice his cultural history of being a Jew in order to enter other cultural circumstances to reach people with the Gospel. However, he specifically stated that he never sacrificed the "*law to God,*" as he was always "*under the law to Christ*" (I Corinthians 9:21). You must be willing to use your cultural circumstances to advance the Gospel. Therefore, You must commit to never honor or engage in cultural activities that dishonor God. But at the same time, you must purposefully participate in your current culture in ways that God is not dishonored so that you can represent Him to those around you

Walking Where You Are Called in Your Employment

In I Corinthians 7:21-24, Paul presented his third circumstance within which believers should be representing Christ, saying, "*Art thou called being a servant? care not for it: but if thou mayest be made free, use it rather. For he that is called in the Lord, being a servant, is the Lord's freeman: likewise also he that is called, being free, is Christ's servant. Ye are bought with a price; be not ye the servants of men. Brethren, let every man, wherein he is called, therein abide with God.*" Although employment has replaced servanthood today, Paul's instruction is still relevant. Every believer is to use his place of employment and a good work ethic to further the name of Christ. In Ephesians 6:5-9, Paul wrote to both employees and employers, saying, "*Servants, be obedient to them that are your masters according to the flesh, with fear and trembling, in singleness of your heart, as unto Christ; Not with eyeservice, as menpleasers; but as the servants of Christ, doing the will of God from the heart; With good will doing service, as to the Lord, and not to men: Knowing that whatsoever good thing any man doeth, the same shall he receive of the Lord, whether he be bond or free. And, ye masters, do the same things unto them, forbearing threatening: knowing that your Master also is in heaven; neither is there respect of persons with him.*" Therefore, when God allows you to labor under human authority, you are to do so as if you are working for God Himself. Also, if God allows you to labor over others, you are to do so, remembering that God is over you. Although there is no sin in looking for new employment, each and every job must be done while "*abiding with God*" by working "*as to the Lord*" and representing Him to those who work with you (I Corinthians 7:24, Ephesians 6:7).

Walking Where You Are Called Is a Personal Choice

Paul's teaching in I Corinthians 7:10-24 is clear: no matter where you find yourself within your family, your culture, or your employment, you are to live as a child of God who represents Him

The Christian's Walk

to those around you. Are you living within the privacy of your own home in such a way that Jesus Christ is being represented to your family members? Are you living within your society in such a way that you invite those around you to learn of Christ while rejecting cultural activities that dishonor God's Word? Are you representing God the Father and the Lord Jesus Christ in your place of employment, working for God's glory rather than the praise of men? What changes in your family life, cultural participation, or employment must you make to correctly display that you are a child of God in those relationships and responsibilities that God has given you?

The Christian's Walk

Biblical Principles about
Walking Where You Are Called

✓ **II Timothy 2:8-10** - Christians are called by a holy calling.

✓ **Titus 2:11-14** - Christians are to live godly in this present world.

✓ **Ephesians 2:11-22** - Christians, both Jew, and Gentile, are part of God's household.

✓ **Matthew 19:3-9** - God did not design marriage to end in divorce.

✓ **Ephesians 5:22-33** - Christian couples are to represent Christ and the church in their relationship.

✓ **Colossians 3:18-19** - Christian husbands are to be loving, and Christian wives are to be submissive.

✓ **Ephesians 6:4** - Christian parents are not to provoke their children, but rather should lead them in the things of the Lord.

✓ **Colossians 3:21** - Christian parents are not to provoke their children, in order to protect them from discouragement.

✓ **Colossians 3:22-25** - Christian employees are to work for their employers as if they are working for Jesus Christ.

✓ **I Timothy 6:1-3** - Christian employees are to honor their employers.

Walking where You Are Called

- ✓ **Titus 2:9-10** - Christian employees are to obey and work faithfully for their employers.

- ✓ **I Peter 2:18-21** - Christian employees are to be subject to their employers, even when they themselves are not good.

- ✓ _____ - _____

- ✓ _____ - _____

- ✓ _____ - _____

- ✓ _____ - _____

- ✓ _____ - _____

- ✓ _____ - _____

- ✓ _____ - _____

- ✓ _____ - _____

- ✓ _____ - _____

- ✓ _____ - _____

The Christian's Walk

Biblical Investigation about
Walking Where You Are Called

✎ Bible Reading: I Corinthians 7:10-24, Galatians 2:14-16
✎ Bible Memory Verses: I Corinthians 7:17
17 But as God hath distributed to every man, as the Lord hath called every one, so let him walk. And so ordain I in all churches.

1. Walking where you are called is a lifestyle of <u>godliness</u> within your already-established <u>relationships</u> and <u>responsibilities</u>.

2. What have you been called to be when you believed in Jesus Christ as your personal Savior? (I Corinthians 1:2, 9, 24, 26)
   a   To be <u>a saint</u>
   b   To be <u>in the fellowship of Jesus Christ</u>
   c   To be <u>brethren (family, regardless of my nationality)</u>

3. Whose family did you join when you believed in Jesus Christ as your personal Savior? (John 1:12, I John 3:1-3, I Peter 2:9-10)
   <u>God's</u>
   ☞ ?What are some blessings that come from being a part of God's family?

4. What are the three circumstances in which you are to live according to your spiritual calling? (I Corinthians 7:10-24)
   a   In my <u>family</u>
   b   In my <u>culture</u>
   c   In my <u>employment</u>

Walking where You Are Called

With whom are you to abide in each of the above circumstances?
<u>God</u>

5. Have you been called to live separate from the unsaved? (I Corinthians 5:9-11, Philippians 2:15-16)
Yes / No
How are you to live while living in the midst of the unsaved?
a   <u>Blameless</u>
b   <u>Harmless</u>
☞ ?What are a few examples of how you can live correctly in the midst of the unsaved?
_____
_____

6. How did the early church walk in their daily activities? (Acts 9:31)
<u>In the fear of the Lord and in the comfort of the Holy Ghost</u>
What happened to the number of believers because of their godly testimony to their community?
<u>It was multiplied</u>
☞ What are some ways that you might walk in the fear of God in your daily activities?
_____
_____

7. Did Jesus pray that you would be taken out of the world? (John 17:15)
Yes / No
From what did Jesus pray that you would be kept?
<u>Evil</u>

The Christian's Walk

☞ What evil things does the lost world around you do that Jesus wants you to be kept away from?

_____

_____

Walking Where You Are Called in Your Family

8. Is it God's will that a marriage be broken up? (I Corinthians 7:10-17, Malachi 2:14-16)
    Yes / No
    Should a saved spouse leave his or her unsaved spouse?
    Yes / No
    How should a saved spouse respond if an unsaved spouse desires to leave?
    Let the person go in peace
    What are the benefits of staying with an unsaved spouse?
    a   The possible salvation of the spouse
    b   The possible salvation of the children
    ☞ How can these principles apply in your relationships with your other unsaved family members?

    _____

    _____

9. How should a wife respond when her husband does not obey God's Word? (I Peter 3:1-7)
    Live with her husband in submission and a meek and quiet spirit

    How should a husband respond when his wife does not obey God's Word?
    Live with his wife according to knowledge and treat her with honor

Study Guide - Page 141

☞ What are some examples of how you can live godly even when your spouse chooses to disobey God's Word?
_____
_____

Walking Where You Are Called in Your Culture

10. Does your salvation remove your cultural distinctions? (I Corinthians 7:17-20, 1:22-24)
    Yes / No
    Do your cultural distinctions affect your value to God?
    Yes / No
    What must you keep regardless of your cultural traditions?
    The commandments of God

11. How must each person accept God's salvation regardless of his or her culture? (Romans 3:29-30, Galatians 2:14-16, 5:6, 6:15, II Corinthians 5:17, I Corinthians 1:22-24)
    By faith
    What did God make you at your salvation, regardless of your culture?
    A new creature

12. Should you be willing to set aside your cultural distinctions in order to reach others with the Gospel? (I Corinthians 9:20-23)
    Yes / No
    Whose law are you under, regardless of your culture?
    The law of Christ
    ☞ Is cultural tradition a reason to disobey God's Word?
    Yes / No

The Christian's Walk

☞ What are some cultural traditions that you should not participate in because they might violate God's Word?

_____
_____

Walking Where You Are Called in Your Employment

13. Whose servant are you, regardless of your employment? (I Corinthians 7:21-24)
    Christ's
    ☞ What are some ways in which you can work as Christ's servant while being employed by another employer?

    _____
    _____

14. How are you to work for your employer? (Ephesians 6:5-9)
    5 Servants, be <u>obedient</u> to them that are your masters according to the flesh, with <u>fear</u> and <u>trembling</u>, in <u>singleness</u> of your <u>heart</u>, as unto <u>Christ</u>;
    6 Not with <u>eyeservice</u>, as <u>menpleasers</u>; but as the <u>servants</u> of <u>Christ</u>, doing the <u>will</u> of <u>God</u> from the <u>heart</u>;
    7 With good <u>will</u> doing <u>service</u>, as to the <u>Lord</u>, and not to <u>men</u>:
    Who will receive your good work for your employer?
    The Lord
    ☞ As an employee, what are some good works that you can fulfill regardless of your employer's knowledge or praise?

    _____

    As an employer, what are you to forbear?
    Threatening
    As an employer, Who is your master?
    God

Walking where You Are Called

Is God a respecter of persons between an employer and employee?
Yes / No

☞ As an employer, what are some ways that you can represent your spiritual master to your employees?

_____
_____

Walking Where You Are Called
Is a Personal Choice

15. Are there areas of your life that should be changed so you can be walking where you are called? What are those areas, and what changes should you make? Will you ask God for His help to make these changes?

_____
_____
_____
_____
_____
_____
_____
_____
_____
_____
_____
_____
_____
_____
_____

Personal Notes about
Walking Where You Are Called

Chapter 8

Walking with Them That Are Without

Colossians 4:5-6
5 Walk in wisdom toward them that are without,
redeeming the time.
6 Let your speech be alway with grace,
seasoned with salt,
that ye may know how ye ought to answer every man.

I Thessalonians 4:11-12
11 And that ye study to be quiet,
and to do your own business,
and to work with your own hands,
as we commanded you;
12 That ye may walk honestly
toward them that are without,
and that ye may have lack of nothing.

Chapter 8

Walking with Them That Are Without

Colossians 4:5-6
I Thessalonians 4:12

A Biblical Instruction about Walking with Them That Are Without

In Colossians 4:5-6 and I Thessalonians 4:12, the apostle Paul instructed the New Testament believers to be purposeful in how they interact with those around them, saying, *"walk…toward them that are without."* Several times throughout the New Testament, the phrase "them that are without" distinguishes those who believe in Christ and have eternal life with those who do not. In Mark 4:11, Jesus, while answering His disciples' question about His use of parables, said, *"Unto you it is given to know the mystery of the kingdom of God: but unto them that are without, all these things are done in parables."* Jesus was indicating that because His disciples believed in and followed Him, they were different from those who did not. As discussed in chapter five, "Walking in the Light," every believer is called out of the world's darkness into God's light at the moment of their salvation (Ephesians 5:8). For this reason, Jesus could say in John 17:14-15, *"I have given them thy [God the Father's] word; and the world hath hated them, because they are not of the world, even as I am not of the world. I pray not that thou shouldest take them out of the world, but that thou shouldest keep them from the evil."* Therefore, Paul's use of the phrase indicates that believers are to recognize that they have been separated from the world and thus must live distinct from the world.

In I Corinthians 5:12, Paul used the phrase to distinguish those who were believers and part of the local church from those who were not, saying, *"For what have I to do to judge them also that are without? do not ye judge them that are within?"* In the context, Paul was helping the local church recognize its role in lovingly correcting a sinful believer who had been made separate from the world by God at salvation but was choosing to live as if he were still part of the world. Paul once again used the phrase in I Timothy 3:7 while giving the qualifications of a pastor, saying, *"Moreover he must have a good report of them which are without; lest he fall into reproach and the snare of the devil."* Within this context, Paul taught that a pastor must be especially careful to maintain a godly lifestyle before the unsaved so that there is no opportunity for the devil to attack his personal testimony or ministry.

Paul's use of the phrase *"walk...toward them that are without"* indicates that believers have been separated from the world and must maintain a distinct. More specifically, in Colossians 4:5, he said they are to *"walk in wisdom."* In I Thessalonians 4:12, he said they are to *"walk honestly."* *Walking with them that are without is a lifestyle that reflects a distinction from the world by demonstrating godly wisdom and honesty while interacting with the unsaved.*

Walking Wisely with Them That Are Without
In Colossians 4:5, Paul commanded the believers in Colosse to *"walk in wisdom toward them that are without, redeeming the time."* As believers fulfill their daily activities, they will continually be confronted with the world's philosophies and temptations while at the same time facing rejection when they choose to follow Christ. It is for this reason that Jesus said to His disciples, *"Behold, I send you forth as sheep in the midst of wolves: be ye therefore wise as serpents, and harmless as doves"*

The Christian's Walk

(Matthew 10:16). Although the world is full of knowledge and clever ways to use that knowledge, true wisdom comes from God (James 1:5-8). Previously in Colossians 2:3, while speaking of the greatness of God the Father and of Christ, Paul said, "*In whom are hid all the treasures of wisdom and knowledge.*" God is the source of true wisdom to which you have access when you learn from and about Him. James 3:13-17 explains further by answering the question, "*Who is a wise man and endued with knowledge among you?*" saying, "*Let him shew out of a good conversation his works with meekness of wisdom. But if ye have bitter envying and strife in your hearts, glory not, and lie not against the truth. This wisdom descendeth not from above, but is earthly, sensual, devilish. For where envying and strife is, there is confusion and every evil work. But the wisdom that is from above is first pure, then peaceable, gentle, and easy to be intreated, full of mercy and good fruits, without partiality, and without hypocrisy.*" As you live in this sin-filled world, you are to reject the wicked wisdom of the world, which always leads to sin, and follow after heavenly wisdom that comes from God, which always leads to righteousness. Although the world may publicly reject your righteous living because it shows that you are different, it will also "*be ashamed*" when it "*falsely accuse[s] your good conversation in Christ*" (I Peter 3:16).

Paul concluded his instruction to the believers in Colossians 4:5 with the phrase, "*redeeming the time.*" True wisdom never wastes a minute because it recognizes that life is short (Romans 13:11). Life is short both for the believer to fulfill God's will and for the unbeliever to be saved. As a result, true wisdom diligently seeks to learn and do God's will before time is up (Colossians 1:9). In Ephesians 5:15-17, Paul wrote, "*See then that ye walk circumspectly, not as fools, but as wise, redeeming the time, because the days are evil. Wherefore be ye not unwise, but understanding what the will of the Lord is.*" The reality that life is short and that the world around you is full of wickedness should motivate you to seek God's wisdom more diligently so that you can live more circumspectly, or carefully. To grow in God's wisdom, you must commit to growing in your knowledge of Him through studying His Word. Colossians 3:16 says, "***Let the word of Christ dwell in you richly in all wisdom.***" As you fill your life with God's Word, your heart will be filled with His wisdom. As your heart is filled with God's wisdom, He will become more precious to you, and you will naturally begin to reflect Him more clearly to the lost world around you. And, as you reflect God to the lost world around you, some unbelievers—not all, but some—will begin to inquire why you are different and how they can also enjoy a changed life (I Peter 3:15).

Although your lifestyle, when guided by God's wisdom, reveals to the lost world that you are different, your verbal answer to their questions about why you are different may lead them to accept Christ as their personal Savior. It is for this reason that Paul concluded his teaching about walking wisely with them that are without by saying, "***Let your speech be alway with grace, seasoned with salt, that ye may know how ye ought to answer every man***" (Colossians 4:6). You must allow God's wisdom not only to affect your actions but also to guide your speech. You must seek to learn God's answers to the lost world's questions in order to lead them to enjoy a personal relationship with Him through Christ, just as someone else did for you.

Walking Honestly with Them That Are Without

In I Thessalonians 4:12, Paul encouraged the believers in Thessalonica, writing, "***Walk honestly toward them that are without,…that ye may have lack of nothing.***" As mentioned previously, the believers in Thessalonica were under great persecution. Consequently, Paul was not writing to correct their wrongdoing in the present as much as to prevent them from committing wrongdoing in the future. In this context, Paul was attempting to prevent an attitude of laziness that can develop from a misunderstanding of faith and God's process of providing for one's own needs. He knew that such a misunderstanding would

The Christian's Walk

lead believers to be dishonest or disorderly as they become expectant on others to supply what they should have worked to supply. Paul exhorted the believers to be diligent workers, saying, *"And that ye study to be quiet, and to do your own business, and to work with your own hands, as we commanded you"* (I Thessalonians 4:11). Sadly, some of the believers in Thessalonica did not heed Paul's instruction, and he had to confront them more directly in II Thessalonians 3:6-12, saying, *"Now we command you, brethren, in the name of our Lord Jesus Christ, that ye withdraw yourselves from every brother that walketh disorderly, and not after the tradition which he received of us…For even when we were with you, this we commanded you, that if any would not work, neither should he eat. For we hear that there are some which walk among you disorderly, working not at all, but are busybodies. Now them that are such we command and exhort by our Lord Jesus Christ, that with quietness they work, and eat their own bread."*

Although God promises to provide for your daily needs, He often requires your participation in the process (Matthew 6:25-34). Paul often worked to supply his own needs, even while being actively involved in ministry. In I Thessalonians 2:9, he wrote, *"Ye remember, brethren, our labour and travail: for labouring night and day, because we would not be chargeable unto any of you, we preached unto you the gospel of God."* He also added in II Thessalonians 3:7-9, *"For yourselves know how ye ought to follow us: for we behaved not ourselves disorderly among you; Neither did we eat any man's bread for nought; but wrought with labour and travail night and day, that we might not be chargeable to any of you: Not because we have not power, but to make ourselves an ensample unto you to follow us."* Paul was a tentmaker and used his craft to support himself and others (Acts 18:1-3, 20:33-35). His laboring, while sharing the Gospel, serves as an example of how you should work diligently for your own physical needs and share the Gospel to meet the spiritual needs of the lost around you. However, if you are not diligent in your

Walking with Them That Are Without

physical labor, you can expect that your spiritual message will not go far. Your work ethic and your spiritual ethic must match. You must be diligent in every area of your daily physical and spiritual responsibilities while trusting God for the results.

Walking with Them That Are Without Is a Personal Choice

Paul's teaching about walking with them that are without indicates that your spiritual testimony is affected by your daily conduct. Are you seeking God for His wisdom in your daily interactions with those around you? Are you using your time wisely to do God's will amid this wicked world? Are you committed to seeking God's will by studying His Word? Are you preparing to wisely answer the question of those asking you about your godly lifestyle? Are you working honestly, or diligently, to provide for your own needs? Are you using your work ethic to extend the Gospel message? What changes must you make in your life so that you can walk in wisdom and honesty before the lost world around you?

The Christian's Walk

Biblical Principles about Walking with Them That Are Without

- ✓ **John 15:18-21** - God has separated Christians from the world, which is why the world does not accept them.

- ✓ **I John 4:4-6** - Christians have overcome the world through their relationship with Jesus Christ.

- ✓ **Romans 11:33-36** - God's wisdom is beyond human comprehension.

- ✓ **I Corinthians 3:18-20** - God's wisdom makes the world's wisdom look like foolishness.

- ✓ **Ephesians 1:3-12** - God provides Christians with abundant wisdom through Jesus Christ.

- ✓ **Ephesians 1:15-20** - Christians are to pray that their fellow believers may grow in wisdom through their knowledge of God the Father.

- ✓ **Romans 13:13** - A Christian's entire life should be characterized by honesty (decency).

- ✓ **I Corinthians 14:40** - All things in the local church are to be done decently (honestly).

- ✓ **Ephesians 4:28** - Christians are to work with their own hands with the intention of helping those in need.

- ✓ **II Corinthians 8:21** - Christians are to live honestly before God and all men.

Walking with Them That Are Without

✓ **I Peter 2:11-12** - Christians are to live honestly even when the lost speaks evil of them.

✓ _____ - _____

✓ _____ - _____

✓ _____ - _____

✓ _____ - _____

✓ _____ - _____

✓ _____ - _____

✓ _____ - _____

✓ _____ - _____

✓ _____ - _____

✓ _____ - _____

✓ _____ - _____

The Christian's Walk

Biblical Investigation about
Walking with Them That Are Without

✎ Bible Reading: Colossians 4:5-6, I Thessalonians 4:11-12
✎ Bible Memory Verses: Colossians 4:5-6
> *5 Walk in wisdom toward them that are without, redeeming the time.*
> *6 Let your speech be alway with grace, seasoned with salt, that ye may know how ye ought to answer every man.*

1. Walking with them that are without is a lifestyle that reflects a <u>distinction</u> from the world by demonstrating godly <u>wisdom</u> and <u>honesty</u> while interacting with the <u>unsaved</u>.

2. Who are those classified as being "without?" (Colossians 4:5-6, I Thessalonians 4:12, Mark 4:11, I Corinthians 5:12, I Timothy 3:7)
   <u>Unbelievers</u>
   ☞ List a few people who you know are currently unbelievers but with whom you interact regularly.
   _____
   _____

3. What does "not being part of this world" mean? (John 17:14-16)
   <u>To be living in the physical world but not being part of the world's spiritual system</u>

Walking Wisely
with Them That Are Without

4. How are you to live with them that are without? (Colossians 4:5)
   In wisdom

5. Because there are spiritual danger's all around you, how are you to live? (Matthew 10:16)
   16 Behold, I send you forth as sheep in the midst of <u>wolves</u>: be ye therefore <u>wise</u> as serpents, and <u>harmless</u> as doves.
   ☞ What are some of the spiritual dangers that you face every day?

6. Who can provide you with true wisdom? (James 1:5-8)
   God
   What must you do to receive true wisdom?
   Ask God in faith

7. In Whom can be found the treasures of wisdom and knowledge? (Colossians 2:2-3)
   In God the Father and Jesus Christ

8. What is the proof that a person is wise? (James 3:13-17)
   His conversation (lifestyle) produces works with meekness
   What words describe earthly, sensual, and devilish wisdom?
   a Bitter envying
   b Strife
   ☞ In what areas of your life has earthly wisdom caused conflicts, and what should you do to correct it?

The Christian's Walk

What words describe heavenly wisdom?
a Pure
b Peaceable
c Gentle
d Easy to be entreated
e Full of mercy
f Full of good fruits
g Without partiality
h Without hypocrisy

☞ What are some areas in your life in which you can grow in applying heavenly wisdom?

9. Who will be ashamed when your conversation (lifestyle) reflects Jesus Christ and the world makes false accusations against you? (I Peter 3:16)
The false accusers

10. What will you do with your time if you walk in wisdom? (Colossians 4:5)
Redeem it
☞ What are some ways that you could improve the use of your time?

11. How are you walking if you do not redeem your time? (Ephesians 5:15-17)
As a fool
Why must you be careful to redeem your time?
Because the days are evil

Walking with Them That Are Without

What will you seek to learn and obey when you walk in wisdom?
<u>God's will</u>

12. What must dwell in your heart if you are going to walk in wisdom? (Colossians 3:16)
    <u>The Word of Christ - The Bible</u>
    ☞ What can you do to ensure that God's Word dwells in your heart?

13. As you walk in wisdom, knowing and obeying God's will, based on His Word, what must you also be ready to do for the lost around you? (I Peter 3:15)
    <u>Be ready to answer their questions about my spiritual hope</u>

14. What word should describe your speech as you walk in wisdom? (Colossians 4:6)
    <u>Grace</u>
    ☞ What are some subjects that the lost world around you might ask you about?

    ☞ What are some ways that you could better prepare yourself for the above subjects?

Walking Honestly
with Them That Are Without

15. How are you to live with them that are without? (I Thessalonians 4:12)
    Honestly - orderly
    What will you lack if you live honestly?
    Nothing

16. How should you fulfill your personal responsibilities? (I Thessalonians 4:11)
    11 And that ye study to be <u>quiet</u>, and to do your own <u>business</u>, and to work with your own <u>hands</u>, as we commanded you;
    ☞ What are some areas of your life in which you may be more concerned about how others work rather than in fulfilling your own responsibilities?

    _____
    _____

17. What should you not do if you do not work? (II Thessalonians 3:6-12)
    Eat
    In this passage, what does it mean to walk disorderly?
    To not work and to be a busybody
    How should you work so that you are not walking disorderly?
    Quietly
    Whose bread should you eat?
    My own

18. What has God promised to provide you when you obey Him? (Matthew 6:25-34)
    All things that I truly need

19. When did Paul work to provide for his own needs? (I Thessalonians 2:9, II Thessalonians 3:7-9)
    <u>Night and day</u>
    What did Paul preach to those who would listen?
    <u>The Gospel of God</u>
    ☞ How might your diligence in your work positively or negatively affect your ability to share the Gospel with the lost around you?

20. Besides providing for your own needs, why should you work? (Acts 18:1-3, 20:33-35)
    <u>To support the weak</u>
    ☞ How can you use the resources you have earned by working to help reach the unsaved with the Gospel?

    What is more blessed than receiving?
    <u>Giving</u>
    ☞ When was the last time you gave a gift to someone for no reason other than that they had a legitimate need and you could help supply for that need?

Walking with Them That Are Without
Is a Personal Choice

21. Are there areas of your life that should be changed so you can be walking in wisdom and honesty with them that are without? What are those areas, and what changes should you make? Will you ask God for His help to make these changes?

_____
_____
_____
_____
_____
_____
_____
_____
_____
_____
_____
_____
_____
_____
_____
_____
_____
_____
_____
_____
_____
_____
_____
_____
_____
_____

The Christian's Walk

Personal Notes about
Walking with Them That Are Without

Chapter 9

Walking after an Example
Walking by the Same Rule
Walking with the Same Mind
Walking in the Same Spirit

Philippians 3:8-19
16 Nevertheless, whereto we have already attained,
let us walk by the same rule,
let us mind the same thing.
17 Brethren, be followers together of me,
and mark them which walk
so as ye have us for an ensample.
18 (For many walk,
of whom I have told you often,
and now tell you even weeping,
that they are the enemies of the cross of Christ:
19 Whose end is destruction, whose God is their belly,
and whose glory is in their shame,
who mind earthly things.)

II Corinthians 12:14-19
18 I desired Titus, and with him I sent a brother. Did Titus make a gain of you? walked we not in the same spirit? walked we not in the same steps?

II Thessalonians 3:6-15

6 Now we command you, brethren,
in the name of our Lord Jesus Christ,
that ye withdraw yourselves
from every brother that walketh disorderly,
and not after the tradition which he received of us.
7 For yourselves know how ye ought to follow us:
for we behaved not ourselves disorderly among you;
8 Neither did we eat any man's bread for nought;
but wrought with labour and travail night and day,
that we might not be chargeable to any of you:
9 Not because we have not power,
but to make ourselves an ensample unto you
to follow us.
10 For even when we were with you,
this we commanded you, that if any would not work,
neither should he eat.
11 For we hear that there are some
which walk among you disorderly,
working not at all, but are busybodies.

Chapter 9

Walking after an Example
Walking by the Same Rule
Walking with the Same Mind
Walking in the Same Spirit

Philippians 3:8-19
II Corinthians 12:14-19
II Thessalonians 3:6-15

A Biblical Instruction about Walking after an Example

In Philippians 3:8-14, the apostle Paul shared his personal goal for his spiritual walk, saying, *"Yea doubtless, and I count all things but loss for the excellency of the knowledge of Christ Jesus my Lord...That I may know him, and the power of his resurrection, and the fellowship of his sufferings, being made conformable unto his death; If by any means I might attain unto the resurrection of the dead. Brethren, I count not myself to have apprehended: but this one thing I do, forgetting those things which are behind, and reaching forth unto those things which are before, I press toward the mark for the prize of the high calling of God in Christ Jesus."* Paul was passionate about growing in his knowledge of and obedience to Jesus Christ. He humbly realized that he had not yet learned or adequately applied all that he needed to. However, he was dedicated to taking steps forward in his spiritual pursuit.

In Philippians 3:15-17, Paul encouraged the believers in Philippi to join him in his passion and pursuit of knowing and

Walking after an Example

living for Christ, saying, "*Let us therefore, as many as be perfect, be thus minded...let us walk by the same rule, let us mind the same thing. Brethren, be followers together of me, and mark them which walk so as ye have us for an ensample.*" Paul's life was guided by one primary rule: knowing and pleasing Christ at all costs. That is the same rule, or way of thinking, that all perfect, or mature, believers must maintain. Paul, while speaking to the believers in Corinth, revealed that he was not alone in his dedication to putting Christ and His ministry before one's personal desires, saying, "*I desired Titus, and with him I sent a brother. Did Titus make a gain of you? walked we not in the same spirit? walked we not in the same steps?*" (II Corinthians 12:18). Although your life's circumstances are different from Paul's, Timothy's, and that of the unnamed brother, their dedication to serving Christ in each of life's events should be an encouragement to you to do the same. *Walking after an example is a lifestyle that recognizes and learns from other Christ-centered believers.*

Walking after an Example Requires Learning from Christ-centered Believers

In Philippians 3:17, Paul began his command to follow godly examples by calling the believers in Philippi "*brethren,*" as he did numerous other times throughout his letter (Philippians 1:12, 14, 3:1, 3:13, 4:1, 8). Paul did not believe himself to be set apart from his fellow believers but rather recognized that they were all equals as God's children. However, like in any family, he also recognized that being older in the faith, his years of experience and personal testimony could serve as a guide to his younger brothers and sisters in Christ. In this role as an older brother in Christ, Paul commanded his spiritual siblings, saying, "*Be followers together of me, and mark them which walk so as ye have us for an ensample*" (Philippians 3:17). He also added in Philippians 4:9, "*Those things, which ye have both learned, and received, and heard, and seen in me, do: and the God of peace shall be with you.*"

The Christian's Walk

Paul had just explained that his goal was to know and follow Christ. Therefore, his command for other believers to follow him was not given out of pride but rather out of a desire to help those in need. In I Corinthians 11:1, he said, "***Be ye followers of me, even as I also am of Christ.***" After his salvation, Paul's entire life and ministry were focused on Christ. For this reason, he wrote earlier in his letter, "***And I, brethren, when I came to you, came not with excellency of speech or of wisdom, declaring unto you the testimony of God. For I determined not to know any thing among you, save Jesus Christ, and him crucified***" (I Corinthians 2:1-2). He later wrote in II Corinthians 4:2-5, "***But [I] have renounced the hidden things of dishonesty, not walking in craftiness, nor handling the word of God deceitfully....For we preach not ourselves, but Christ Jesus the Lord; and ourselves your servants for Jesus' sake.***" Paul did not desire to make disciples that would follow him; he desired to make disciples of Jesus Christ. Therefore, he concluded his command by saying, "***and mark them which walk so as ye have us for an ensample***" (Philippians 3:17). Paul desired that the believers in Philippi would search for other godly examples they could follow. Some of their examples could come from Bible characters, some from church history, and some from their own local church (Romans 15:4-6, Ephesians 4:11-16). No matter the source, each example needed to be like Paul in their focus on knowing and obeying Christ.

Walking after an Example Requires Separating from Self-centered Believers

In Philippians 3:18-19, Paul warned the Philippian believers of self-centered examples that would distract them from focusing on Christ, saying, "***For many walk, of whom I have told you often, and now tell you even weeping, that they are the enemies of the cross of Christ: Whose end is destruction, whose God is their belly, and whose glory is in their shame, who mind earthly things.***" Unfortunately, even in Paul's day, there were examples of ungodly people who were beginning to have an influence on the believers in Philippi. These influences brought tears to Paul's eyes as they took their focus off Christ and put it on themselves. He also knew that he needed to publicly confront such ungodliness so that other sincere believers would not be tricked by their wicked example.

In II Thessalonians 3:6-15, Paul also publicly addressed those believers who were self-centered rather than Christ-centered, saying, *"Now we command you, brethren, in the name of our Lord Jesus Christ, that ye withdraw yourselves from every brother that walketh disorderly, and not after the tradition which he received of us. For yourselves know how ye ought to follow us: for we behaved not ourselves disorderly among you…to make ourselves an ensample unto you to follow us…For we hear that there are some which walk among you disorderly, working not at all, but are busybodies…And if any man obey not our word by this epistle, note that man, and have no company with him, that he may be ashamed. Yet count him not as an enemy, but admonish him as a brother."* Paul had been very careful to live godly when he was with the Thessalonian believers so as to supply them with an example of biblical Christianity (I Thessalonians 2:9-10). Many believers in Thessalonica appreciated and followed Paul's example, but some were not following his example and had become lazy and carnal (I Thessalonians 1:6). Therefore, Paul felt it necessary to remind the believers to follow his example and to separate from those who were not. Such a separation was not to be done to be harsh but rather to admonish or encourage those disobedient believers to repent of their self-focus and return to a Christ-focus.

Walking after an Example Is a Personal Choice

The New Testament's teaching about walking while following other Christ-centered believers commands you to find godly believers who help guide you to grow in your knowledge and obedience to Christ. It also commands you to separate

The Christian's Walk

yourself from self-centered believers who will distract you from knowing and living for Christ. Are you purposefully looking for and studying about Bible characters to help you gow in your spiritual walk? Are you identifying believers from church history or in your current local church who are Christ-focused and can serve as examples and counselors to guide you to know Christ better? Are you being discerning about those individuals who influence your life, making sure that they are not self-focused? In what areas of your life have you not been a Christ-example for other believers who are watching your life? What changes must you make in your life so that you can both *follow* other Christ-centered examples and *be* a Christ-centered example?

The Christian's Walk

Biblical Principles about Walking after an Example

- ✓ **I John 2:3-5** - A Christian must keep Jesus's commandments in order to display that he truly knows Him.

- ✓ **I Corinthians 9:24-27** - A Christian must be self-controlled while living for Jesus Christ.

- ✓ **Romans 15:5-6** - Like-mindedness comes from God as Christians focus on Jesus Christ.

- ✓ **Hebrews 11:1-12:3** - The accounts of faithful men and women in the Scriptures have been given to encourage Christians to be faithful throughout their lifetime.

- ✓ **I Timothy 4:12** - Christian young people are to be examples to other believers.

- ✓ **I Peter 5:3** - Spiritual leaders are to be examples to those they lead.

- ✓ **Romans 16:17-18** - Christians are to separate from those who cause division and do not follow sound doctrine.

- ✓ _____ - _____

- ✓ _____ - _____

- ✓ _____ - _____

Walking after an Example

- ✓ _____ - _____
- ✓ _____ - _____
- ✓ _____ - _____
- ✓ _____ - _____
- ✓ _____ - _____
- ✓ _____ - _____
- ✓ _____ - _____
- ✓ _____ - _____
- ✓ _____ - _____
- ✓ _____ - _____
- ✓ _____ - _____
- ✓ _____ - _____

The Christian's Walk

Biblical Investigation about Walking after an Example

✎ Bible Reading: Philippians 3:8-19, II Corinthians 12:14-19, II Thessalonians 3:6-15

✎ Bible Memory Verses: Philippians 3:17

17 Brethren, be followers together of me, and mark them which walk so as ye have us for an ensample.

1. Walking after an example is a lifestyle that <u>recognizes</u> and <u>learns</u> from other <u>Christ-centered</u> believers.

2. What should be your primary goal throughout your Christian life? (Philippians 3:8-16, I Corinthians 12:18)
   <u>To grow in my knowledge of Jesus Christ</u>
   What must you do with your past life if you are going to be able to pursue your goal?
   <u>Forget those things which are behind</u>
   What must you do in the future if you are going to reach your goal?
   <u>Press toward the mark</u>
   ☞ What are some ways in which you can display your dedication to grow in your knowledge of Jesus Christ in your day-to-day life?

   _____

   How do perfect or mature Christians walk?
   a   With the same <u>mind</u>
   b   With the same <u>rule</u>

Walking after an Example
Requires Learning from Christ-centered Believers

3. With whom are you to be walking throughout your spiritual life? (Philippians 3:17, 1:12, 14, 3:1, 3:13, 4:1, 8)
   Brethren = other believers
   What are you to do to believers who have the same goal as the apostle Paul?
   Mark them as examples
   ☞ Who are a few godly examples that you can mark and follow?
   _____
   _____

4. What must you do if you are going to follow Paul's example? (Philippians 4:9)
   9 Those things, which ye have both <u>learned</u>, and <u>received</u>, and <u>heard</u>, and <u>seen</u> in me, do: and the God of peace shall be with you.

5. When you are following others, Who must they be following? (I Corinthians 11:1, 2:1-2, II Corinthians 4:2-5)
   Jesus Christ

6. List a few biblical or historical believers who can serve as good examples for your spiritual walk. (Romans 15:4-6)
   _____
   _____

7. What is the purpose of your local church's spiritual leadership? (Ephesians 4:11-16)
   Bring all the believers into the unity of the faith in the body of Jesus Christ

The Christian's Walk

Walking after an Example
Requires Separating from the Self-centered Believers

8. What is the description of those who are not Christ-centered? (Philippians 3:18-19)
   a   Their end is destruction
   b   Their God is their belly
   c   Their glory is in their shame
   d   They mind earthly things

9. What are you to do with those believers who do not follow Paul's example of godliness? (II Thessalonians 3:6-15, 1:6, 2:9-10)
   Separate from them
   What is the purpose of your separation from them?
   To produce shame and admonition for repentance
   ☞ Have you been a bad example to others?
   Yes / No
   ☞ How can you improve your example to others so that they can grow closer to Jesus Christ by following your life?

   ☞ Are there some believers in your life at this time that are a bad example?
   Yes / No
   ☞ How can you limit the influence of these bad examples while admonishing them to live godly in the future?

Walking after an Example
Is a Personal Choice

10. Are there areas of your life that should be changed so you can be walking after an example of a Christ-centered life? What are those areas, and what changes should you make? Will you ask God for His help to make these changes?

_____
_____
_____
_____
_____
_____
_____
_____
_____
_____
_____
_____
_____
_____
_____
_____
_____
_____
_____
_____
_____
_____
_____
_____
_____
_____

Personal Notes about Walking after an Example

Walking after an Example

Chapter 10

Walking in Abundance

I Thessalonians 3:12-4:1
12 And the Lord make you to increase and abound
in love one toward another,
and toward all men,
even as we do toward you:
13 To the end he may stablish your hearts
unblameable in holiness before God, even our Father,
at the coming of our Lord Jesus Christ with all his saints.
1 Furthermore then we beseech you, brethren,
and exhort you by the Lord Jesus,
that as ye have received of us
how ye ought to walk and to please God,
so ye would abound more and more.

Chapter 10

Walking in Abundance

I Thessalonians 3:12-4:1

A Biblical Instruction about Walking in Abundance

In I Thessalonians 4:1, the apostle Paul encouraged the believers in the city of Thessalonica, saying, "*Furthermore then we beseech you, brethren, and exhort you by the Lord Jesus, that as ye have received of us how ye ought to walk and to please God, so ye would abound more and more.*" Paul had only a short time with the new believers in Thessalonica before he was driven away from them by persecution. However, he used his limited time to provide them biblical teaching and a personal example of how they should live their new Christian life (I Thessalonians 2:10-12). In I Thessalonians 2:13-14, Paul praised their initial obedience to his instruction, saying, "*For this cause also thank we God without ceasing, because, when ye received the word of God which ye heard of us, ye received it not as the word of men, but as it is in truth, the word of God, which effectually worketh also in you that believe. For ye, brethren, became followers of the churches of God which in Judaea are in Christ Jesus.*" The believers in Thessalonica started out strong in their new life in Christ, and their faithfulness was beginning to impact other cities. In I Thessalonians 1:6-10, Paul recorded, "*And ye became followers of us, and of the Lord, having received the word in much affliction, with joy of the Holy Ghost: So that ye were ensamples to all that believe in Macedonia and Achaia. For from you sounded out the word of the Lord not only in Macedonia and Achaia, but also in every place your faith to God-ward is spread abroad; so that we need not to speak any thing. For they themselves shew of us what manner of entering in we had unto you, and how ye turned to God from idols to serve the living and true God; And to wait for his Son from heaven, whom he raised from the dead, even Jesus, which delivered us from the wrath to come."*

The believers in Thessalonica believed in God and were sharing their beliefs with those around them. But Paul did not want them to become complacent. He expressed his dependence on Jesus Christ to help them continually increase in their biblical love, which would lead to their living holy before God. He said, *"And the Lord make you to increase and abound in love one towards another, and towards all men, even as we do towards you: to the end he may stablish your hearts unblameable in holiness before God, even our Father, at the coming of our Lord Jesus Christ with all his saints"* (I Thessalonians 3:12-13). *Walking in abundance is a lifestyle that continually increases in love for others and in obedience toward God the Father.*

Walking in Abundance Is Continually Increasing in Love for Others

Chapter five, "Walking in the Light," explained that all believers are to *"walk in love, as Christ also hath loved us"* and that *"all the law is fulfilled in one word, even in this; Thou shalt love thy neighbour as thyself"* (Ephesians 5:2, Galatians 5:14). Although the believers had been loving each other, Paul knew that over time their love could begin to fail by inadvertently offending one another. Paul desired for them to choose to love in abundance and to continually increase in that love so that all the believers' needs would be met. Remember that in chapter two, "Walking Worthy," Ephesians 4:2 revealed that you are to walk worthy of your vocation *"with all lowliness and meekness, with longsuffering, forbearing one another in love."* Therefore, walking in abundance of Christ-like love means walking in abundance in every area of your Christian life.

Once again, it is important to note that Paul was not writing to correct the believers in Thessalonica but rather to encourage them. They had been loving others properly, but that love needed to be constantly growing. So Paul wrote in I Thessalonians 4:9-10, *"But as touching brotherly love ye need not that I write unto you: for ye yourselves are taught of God to love one another. And indeed ye do it toward all the brethren which are in all Macedonia: but we beseech you, brethren, that ye increase more and more."*

Because *"he that loveth another hath fulfilled the law"* as *"love worketh no ill to his neighbour,"* Paul could follow up his encouragement to abound in love by saying, *"For ye know what commandments we gave you by the Lord Jesus. For this is the will of God, even your sanctification, that ye should abstain from fornication... For God hath not called us unto uncleanness, but unto holiness"* (Romans 13:8-10, I Thessalonians 4:2-7). The world will tell you that abounding in love means increasing in sensuality, but God teaches that abounding in love means increasing in purity. Your love for those around you must be a choice to do what is best for them and their spiritual well-being, just as Jesus did for you. Just as Jesus Christ's love for you will never fail no matter how often you neglect or sin against Him, so must your love for others be increasing daily.

Walking in Abundance Is Continually Increasing in Obedience to God

In I Thessalonians 4:1, Paul declared that the goal of the believer's abundant walk is *"to please God."* Therefore, although believers may enjoy growing in their spiritual knowledge and in their relationships with fellow believers, they must always remember that their goal should be to *"do all to the glory of God."* (I Corinthians 10:31). You must never set aside this goal. Instead, you must be dedicated daily to glorify God through your attitudes, actions, and words.

In John 10:10, Jesus Christ said that He came so that you *"might have life, and that [you] might have it more abundantly."* In chapter three, "Walking in Newness of Life," it was revealed that *"where [your] sin abounded, [God's] grace did much more abound"* (Romans 5:20). Additionally, II Corinthians 9:8 declares that God is *"able to make all grace abound toward you; that ye, always having all sufficiency in all things, may abound to every good work."* Romans 15:13 adds that it is God Who can *"fill you with all joy and peace in believing, that ye may abound in hope, through the power of the Holy Ghost."* God has abundantly given you everything you need for this life and eternity. Therefore, it is only reasonable that you should abound in glorifying Him by increasingly obeying His Word in all your daily activities.

Walking in Abundance Is a Personal Choice

I Thessalonians 3:12-4:1 clearly teaches that you are to continually abound in your spiritual life, so much so that it affects your practical living. First, you are to obey God's commands by correctly loving those around you. Second, you are to glorify God by obeying His commands. Are you loving others the way Christ loves you? Are you choosing to do what is best for those around you even when they sin against you? Are you purposefully sanctifying yourself before God so as to protect yourself and those around you from falling into sin? Are you living in such a way that God receives the glory for both your private and public life? Are you growing in your knowledge of God and His Word so that your day-to-day activities can be abundantly pleasing to Him?

The Christian's Walk

Biblical Principles about Walking in Abundance

- ✓ **II Corinthians 1:3-10** - God's comfort abounds when Christians are in abundant tribulation.

- ✓ **Ephesians 1:5-12** - God has given Christians abundant wisdom and prudence.

- ✓ **I Corinthians 15:57-58** - Christians are to be abounding in their work for the Lord.

- ✓ **II Corinthians 8:1-5** - Christians are to be abundant givers.

- ✓ **Colossians 2:6-7** - Christians are to abound in thanksgiving.

- ✓ _____ - _____

- ✓ _____ - _____

- ✓ _____ - _____

- ✓ _____ - _____

- ✓ _____ - _____

- ✓ _____ - _____

Walking in Abundance

- ✓ _____ - _____
- ✓ _____ - _____
- ✓ _____ - _____
- ✓ _____ - _____
- ✓ _____ - _____
- ✓ _____ - _____
- ✓ _____ - _____
- ✓ _____ - _____
- ✓ _____ - _____
- ✓ _____ - _____
- ✓ _____ - _____
- ✓ _____ - _____

The Christian's Walk

Biblical Investigation about Walking in Abundance

✎ Bible Reading: I Thessalonians 3:12-4:7
✎ Bible Memory Verses: I Thessalonians 4:1

1 Furthermore then we beseech you, brethren, and exhort you by the Lord Jesus, that as ye have received of us how ye ought to walk and to please God, so ye would abound more and more.

1. Walking in abundance is a lifestyle that continually <u>increases</u> in <u>love</u> for others and <u>obedience</u> toward God the Father.

2. In what two ways should you abound? (I Thessalonians 4:1)
   a   In how I <u>walk</u>
   b   In how I <u>please</u> God

3. What words should describe your Christian walk if you are going to walk worthy of God? (I Thessalonians 2:10-12)
   a   <u>Holily</u>
   b   <u>Justly</u>
   c   <u>Unblameably</u>

4. How should you receive the ministry of the teaching of God's Word? (I Thessalonians 2:13-14)
   a   <u>As truth</u>
   b   <u>As the word of God</u>
   c   <u>Allowing it to work in me</u>
   ☞ What are some practical ways that you can fulfill the above three responses to God's Word?

5. After you have received the Word of God, what should you do with it? (I Thessalonians 1:6-10)
   <u>Let it be sounded out - share it with others</u>
   ☞ With whom should you share what you are learning from God's Word?
   _____

   Who are you serving when you receive the Word of God and share your faith with others?
   <u>The living and true God</u>

6. What should you allow to abound in your life? (I Thessalonians 3:12-13)
   <u>Love for others</u>
   Who can help you abound in your love for others?
   <u>Jesus Christ</u>
   To what two groups of people should you show love?
   a <u>One to another - believers</u>
   b <u>All men - unbelievers</u>
   ☞ What are some ways you can show your abundant love to the above two groups of people?
   _____

   What is the end goal of loving others?
   <u>That my heart would be unblameable in holiness before God</u>

Walking in Abundance
Is Continually Increasing in Love for Others

7. How are you to love others? (Ephesians 5:2)
   <u>As Christ has loved me</u>
   ☞ Should your love have limitations?
   Yes / No

The Christian's Walk

8. What is fulfilled in biblical love for others? (Galatians 5:14)
    <u>All the law</u>

9. What words described how you will walk when you abound in love for others? (Ephesians 4:2)
    a   <u>Lowliness</u>
    b   <u>Meekness</u>
    c   <u>Longsuffering</u>
    d   <u>Forbearing</u>
    ☞ How have you not been fulfilling the above four descriptions and what should you do about it?

    _____

10. Who teaches you to love others? (I Thessalonians 4:9-10)
    <u>God</u>
    ☞ How has God demonstrated His love for you?

    _____

    In what should you increase more and more?
    <u>Love for others</u>
    ☞ In what ways can you demonstrate your abundant love for others?

    _____

11. What do you owe to others? (Romans 13:8-10)
    <u>To love them</u>
    What will love never do to another person?
    <u>Ill - sin against them or invite them to sin</u>

Walking in Abundance

12. What is God's will for your life? (I Thessalonians 4:2-7)
    <u>My sanctification</u>
    What must you stay away from if you are to live according to God's will?
    <u>Fornication - sensual sin</u>
    ☞ How does the world's love differ from God's love?
    _____
    _____

Walking in Abundance
Is Continually Increasing in Obedience to God

13. For Whose glory should you live? (I Corinthians 10:31)
    <u>God's</u>
    What two normal daily activities should you do for God's glory?
    a <u>Eat</u>
    b <u>Drink</u>
    ☞ What are some other daily activities that you can do for God's glory?
    _____
    _____

14. What type of life does Jesus want you to have? (John 10:10)
    <u>An abundant life</u>

15. What abounded from God when your sin abounded? (Romans 5:20)
    <u>Grace</u>

The Christian's Walk

16. What does God offer you in abundance so that you can abound in good works? (II Corinthians 9:8)
    <u>His grace</u>
    ☞ Because of God's grace, what are some good works that you can abound in doing for Him?
    _____
    _____

17. What does God provide for your daily life? (Romans 15:13)
    13 Now the God of hope fill you with all <u>joy</u> and <u>peace</u> in believing, that ye may abound in <u>hope</u>, through the power of the Holy Ghost.

Walking in Abundance
Is a Personal Choice

18. Are there areas of your life that should change so you can walk in abundance? What are those areas, and what changes should you make? Will you ask God for His help to make these changes?

Personal Notes about Walking in Abundance

Walking in Abundance

Other Ministry Resources Available from Walking in the WORD Ministries

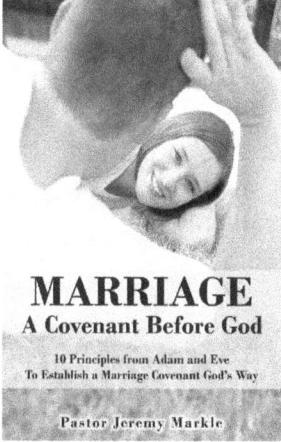

Marriage: A Covenant Before God presents 10 biblical studies about marriage, each one is based on the marital relationship of Adam and Eve and has the purpose of helping young couples understand God's plan and purpose for their life together. Included are practical questions, illustrations, and applications for each biblical truth in order that the couple might grow in their knowledge of each other and how they can glorify God together.

Parenting with Purpose seeks to help young parents to spiritually prepare for the great privilege they have to care for and guide the life of one of God's precious creations. The first three lessons focus on the parents' need to honor God with their child, while the final three lessons focus on the parents' opportunity to represent God the Father to their child.

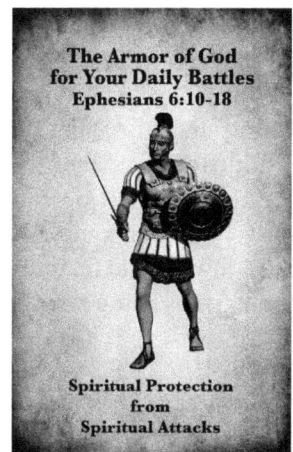

The Armor of God for Your Daily Battles provides a daily Bible study to review the spiritual resources God has provided for each believer so that they can enjoy a victorious Christian life.

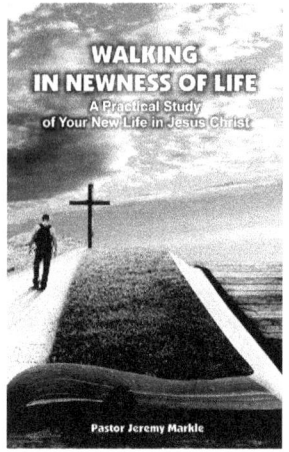

Walking in Newness of Life contains 13 chapters focusing on the privileges that each Christian can enjoy in his "new life" found in Jesus Christ, and the great promises that each of God's children can enjoy, as well as the great responsibilities he must fulfill as he walks "in newness of life" (Romans 6: 4).
*A study guide is available to be used personally or in a small group.

The Calvary Road: Outline Guide was written to enhance your ability to understand, remember, and apply the important spiritual truths shared by Roy Hession in his book, The Calvary Road. After reading each chapter, you can review its content by filling in the blanks, considering the additional passages provided, and answering the reflection and application questions. Throughout this outline guide there are a few special features to help you focus on the truths being taught.

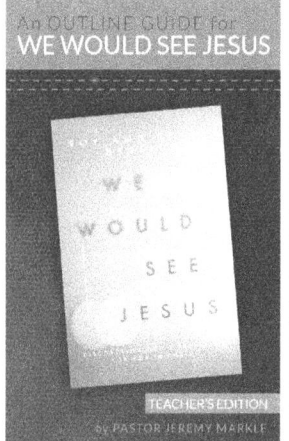

We Would See Jesus: Outline Guide was written to enhance your ability to understand, remember, and apply the important spiritual truths shared by Roy Hession in his book, We Would See Jesus. After reading each chapter, you can review its content by filling in the blanks, considering the additional passages provided, and answering the reflection and application questions. Throughout this outline guide there are a few special features to help you focus on the truths being taught.

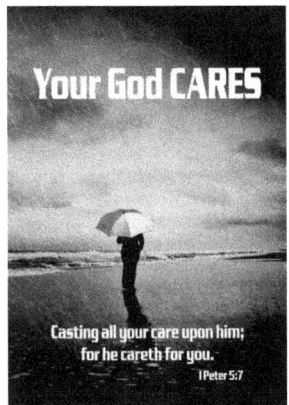

Your God Cares gives biblical hope in time of personal tragedy. It was written following the author's personal experience of living through a natural catastrophe and focuses on God's promise of love and concern for each of our difficulties no mater their size or significance to others. At the end of each chapter there are additional passages of Scripture to present God's promises for the reader's life.

Missions: Ministering Beyond Our Borders was written to provide insight into the physical, emotional, and spiritual adjustments a missionary faces as he begins his new life and ministry. Throughout its pages you will find spiritual encouragements for the missionary and helpful hints for his family and friends who desire to support him in his service to their Lord and Savior Jesus Christ. There is also a "Missionary Edition," which provides a large appendix with additional tips specifically for missionaries.

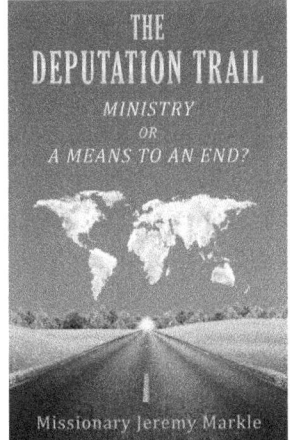

The Deputation Trail: Ministry or a Means to an End? was written to help missionaries during their pre-field ministry by presenting biblically-based philosophies and practical tips to guide them through a God-honoring, church-expanding, and believer-edifying, deputation ministry.

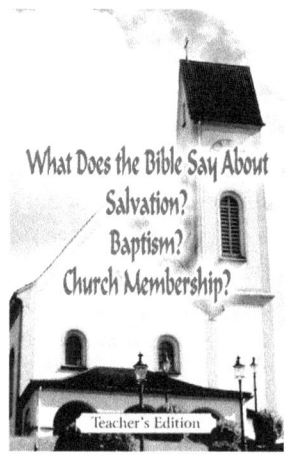

What Does the Bible Say About Salvation, Baptism, and Church Membership? provides a brief Biblical explanation for these three important subjects in the Christian life. Following each study are questions to help review each subject. These studies can be used with a new believer or pre-baptism or pre-church membership classes.

The Heart of Man contains 12 Bible studies about the condition of man's heart and his need to allow God to provide salvation, help him take the first steps of Christian obedience, and give him security in his new relationship with God the Father as one of His children.

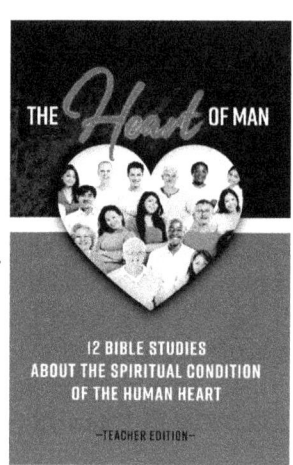

**Please visit
www.walkinginthewordministries.net
to find more biblical resources in English and Spanish.**

www.ingramcontent.com/pod-product-compliance
Lightning Source LLC
Chambersburg PA
CBHW081455040426
42446CB00016B/3256